Peter Gerard

Three meals a day

A diary for the kitchen

Peter Gerard

Three meals a day
A diary for the kitchen

ISBN/EAN: 9783337124465

Printed in Europe, USA, Canada, Australia, Japan

Cover: Foto ©Andreas Hilbeck / pixelio.de

More available books at **www.hansebooks.com**

THREE MEALS A DAY;

A DIARY FOR THE KITCHEN,

—GIVING—

For every day of the year, ac

A BILL OF FAR

BREAKFAST, DINNER

, BY AN OLD EPI

" Variety, in food, is the best appetizer and the

Price: Twenty-fi

FOR SALE BY

GASTRO & CO., 137 E

NEW YORK.
Thos. F. Eagan's Steam Printing
158 East 42d Street.

THREE MEALS A DAY;
A DIARY FOR THE KITCHEN.

JANUARY, 1884.

TUESDAY 1st.

BREAKFAST.—Flounders, Mutton Chops, Quails, Sausage, Eggs.

DINNER.—Oysters on half shell, Beef Soup, Oyster Crab Patties, Salmon Trout, Turkey, Scorzonera Sprouts Salad, Roquefort Chesse, Plum Pudding, Ice Cream.

SUPPER.—Jugged Hare, Sheep's Feet, Sardines and Potato Salad, Munster Cheese, Apricot Marmalade and Cake.

WEDNESDAY 2d.

BREAKFAST.—Blue Fish, Boiled Veal Cutlets, Scrappel, Eggs on Toast.

DINNER.—Shelled Bean Soup, Chicken Croquettes, Haddock, Leg of Mutton, Turnip Sprouts Salad, American Cream Cheese, Custard Pie.

SUPPER.—Meat Croquettes, Pig's Feet, Strasburg fat Liver, Crab Salad, Schweizer Cheese, Stoned Cherries and Cake.

THURSDAY 3d.

BREAKFAST.—Weak Fish, Beefsteak, Pigeons, Head Cheese, Omelette.

DINNER.—Oysters on half shell, Onion Soup, Sweet-bread Patties, White Fish, Chicken, Endive Salad, Gruyere Cheese, Mince Meat Pie.

SUPPER.—Boned Woodcock Pie, Calf's Head, Chicken Salad, Roquefort Choese, Sliced Oranges and Cake.

FRIDAY 4th.

BREAKFAST.—Fish Croquettes, Eels, Boned Herrings and Fried Eggs.

DINNER.—Oyster Stew, Devilled Crabs, Cured Cod Fish, Red Cabbage Salad, Neufchatel Cheese, Rice Pudding.

SUPPER.—Clam Fritters, Macaroni, Eggs on Toast, Herring Salad, Roasted Chestnuts, Munster Cheese, Quince Marmalade and Cake.

SATURDAY 5th.

BREAKFAST.—King Fish, Veal Cutlets, Snipes, Sausage, Eggs.

DINNER.—Julienne Soup, Oyster Patties, Black Bass, Pork and Sour Kraut, Succory Salad, Cheese Pie.

SUPPER.—Meat Croquettes, Wild Rabbit Pie, Pickled Salmon and Potato Salad, Camembert Cheese, Apple Jelly and Cake.

SUNDAY 6th.

BREAKFAST.—Shrimps Patties, Liver and Bacon, Sweet-breads, Eggs.

DINNER.—Oysters on shell, Beef Soup, Vole-au-vent, Sheep's Head, Pheasants, Lettuce Salad, Roquefort Cheese, Plum Pudding, Ice Cream.

SUPPER.—Chicken Croquettes, Meat Jelly, Lobster Salad, Parmesant Cheese, Sliced Oranges and Cake.

MONDAY 7th.

BREAKFAST.—Boiled Fresh Mackerel, Beefsteak, Sausage, Omelette.
DINNER.—Split-Pea Soup, Kidneys, Pike, Fresh boiled Beef, Cauliflower, Brie Cheese, Apple Pie.
SUPPER.—Fried Oysters, Calf's Feet, Anchovy Salad, American Cream Cheese, S oned Cherries and Cake.

TUESDAY 8th.

BREAKFAST.—Co l Fish Tongues, Mutton Chops, Pig's Liver, Ham and Eggs.
DINNER.—Clam Soup, Quails, Fresh Cod Fish, Roast Beef, Corn Salad, Gruyere Cheese, Currant Jelly Pie.
SUPPER.—Mutton Stew, Omelette, Boiled Beef Salad, Munster Cheese, Prunes and Cake.

WEDNESDAY 9th.

BREAKFAST.—Blue Fish, Porksteaks, Fresh Beef's Tongue, Boiled Eggs.
DINNER.—Shelled-Bean Soup, Chicken Croquettes, Sheep's Head, Leg of Mutton, Water Cress Salad, Schweizer Cheese, Coconaut Pie.
SUPPER.—Meat Croquettes, Pig's Feet, Fresh Fish Salad, Emmenthal Cheese, Raspberry Jelly and Cake.

THURSDAY 10th.

BREAKFAST.—Weak Fish, Beefsteak, Head Cheese, Sausage, Omelette.
DINNER.—Oysters on half shell, Onion Soup, Sweet-bread Patties, White Fish, Chicken, Succory Salad, American Cream Cheese, Minoe Meat Pie.
SUPPER.—Wild Rabbit Pie, Smoked Beef Tongue, Chicken Salad, Roquefort Cheese. Sliced Oranges and Cake.

FRIDAY 11th.

BREAKFAST.—Fish Croquettes, Yellow Cat Fish, Boned Herrings and Fried Eggs
DINNER.—Oyster Stew, Devilled Crabs, Cured Cod Fish, Cauliflower, Neufchatel Cheese, Apple Dumplings.
SUPPER.—Clam Fritters, Macaroni, Eggs on Toast, Herring Salad, Gruyere Cheese, Roasted Chestnuts, Cranberry Jelly and Cake.

SATURDAY 12th.

BREAKFAST.—Eels, Broiled Veal Cutlets, White Sausage, Omelette.
DINNER.—Julienne Soup, Oyster Pie, Fresh Salmon, Roast Lamb, Corn Salad, Cheese Pie.
SUPPER.—Meat Croquettes, Pickled Mackerel, Potatoe Salad, Camembert Cheese, Green Winter Berries and Cake.

SUNDAY 13th.

BREAKFAST.—Shrimp Patties, Liver and Bacon, Sweet-breads, Eggs.
DINNER.—Oysters on Shell, Beef Soup, Vole-au-vent, Lake Trout, Canvas-back Duck, Lettuce Salad, Roquefort Cheese, Plum Pudding, Ice Cream.
SUPPER.—Chicken Croquettes, Meat Jelly, Lobster Salad, Camembert Cheese, Sliced Oranges and Cake.

JANUARY, MONDAY 14th.

BREAKFAST.—Boiled Fresh Mackerel, Beefsteak, Sausage, Omelet.

DINNER.—Split-Pea Soup, Wild Duck Pie, Pike, Fresh Boiled Beef, Cole Slaw, Brie Cheese, Apple Pie.

SUPPER.—Fried Oysters, Quails, Head Cheese, Scrambled Eggs, Celery Salad, Roquefort Cheese, Stoned Cherries and Cake.

TUESDAY 15th.

BREAKFAST.—Scallops, Mutton Chops, Pig's Feet, Ham and Eggs.

DINNER.—Green Turtle Soup, Oyster Crab Patties, Fresh Cod Fish, Roast Beef, Corn Salad, Gruyere Cheese, Cranberry Pie.

SUPPER.—Jugged Hare, Sheep's Feet, Omelet, Succory Salad, Munster Cheese, Prunes and Cake.

WEDNESDAY 16th.

BREAKFAST.—Blue Fish, Porksteak, Snipes, Scrapple, Boiled Eggs.

DINNER.—Shelled Bean Soup, Chicken Croquettes, Ray, Leg of Mutton, Scorzonera Sprouts Salad, Schweizer Cheese, Stoned Cherry Pie.

SUPPER.—Meat Croquettes, Calf's Feet, Cold Ham, Crab Salad, Emmenthal Cheese, Raspberry Jelly and Cake.

THURSDAY 17th.

BREAKFAST.—Weak Fish, Beefsteak, Head Cheese, Sausage, Omelet.

DINNER.—Oysters on shell, Onion Soup, Kidneys, White Fish, Chicken, Endive Salad, American Cream Cheese, Mince Meat Pie.

SUPPER.—Broiled Porksteak, Sardines, Chicken Salad, Roquefort Cheese, Orange Slices and Cake.

FRIDAY 18th.

BREAKFAST.—Fish Croquettes, Gudgeons, Boned Herrings and Fried Eggs.

DINNER.—Oyster Stew, Devilled Crabs, Cured Cod Fish, Cole Slaw, Neufchatel Cheese, Rice Pudding.

SUPPER.—Clam Fritters, Macaroni, Eggs on Toast, Herring Salad, Roasted Chestnuts, Gruyere Cheese, Green Winter Berries and Cake.

SATURDAY 19th.

BREAKFAST.—Yellow Perch, Broiled Veal Cutlets, Sausage Pudding, Omelet.

DINNER.—Julienne Soup, Oyster Patties, Haddock, Roast Pork, Corn Salad, Cheese Pie.

SUPPER.—Meat Croquettes, Pickled Salmon, Potato Salad, Camembert Cheese, Stewed Dry Pears and Cake.

SUNDAY 20th.

BREAKFAST.—Shrimps Patties, Liver and Bacon, Sweet-breads, Eggs

DINNER.—Oysters on shell, Beef Soup, Vole-au-vent, Black Bass, Filet of Beef, Lettuce Salad, Roquefort Cheese, Plum Pudding, Ice Cream.

SUPPER.—Chicken Croquettes, Meat Jelly, Lobster Salad, Parmesant Cheese, Sliced Oranges and Cake.

JANUARY, MONDAY 21st.

BREAKFAST.—Boiled Fresh Mackerel, Beefsteak, Sausage, Omelet.
DINNER.—Split-Pea Soup, Kidneys, Pike, Fresh Boiled Beef, Cole Slaw, Brie Cheese, Apple. Pie.
SUPPER.—Fried Oysters, Eggs on Toast, Head Cheese, Corn Salad, American Cream Cheese, Blackberry Jelly and Cake.

TUESDAY 22d.

BREAKFAST.—Boiled Fresh Herrings, Mutton Chops, Pig's Feet, Ham and Eggs
DINNER.—Clam Soup, Oyster Crab Patties, Fresh Cod Fish, Roast Beef, Red Cabbage Salad, Gruyere Cheese, Currant Jelly Pie.
SUPPER.—Mutton Stew, Omelet, Boiled Beef Salad, Munster Cheese, Prunes and Cake.

WEDNESDAY 23d.

BREAKFAST.—Blue Fish, Porksteak, Fresh Beef's Tongue, Eggs on Toast.
DINNER.—Shelled Bean Soup, Chicken Croquettes, Rock Fish, Leg of Mutton, Water Cress Salad, Schweizer Cheese, Custard Pie.
SUPPER.—Meat Croquettes, Sheep's Feet, Strasburg fat Liver, Fresh Fish Salad, Emmenthal Cheese, Currant Jelly and Cake.

THURSDAY 24th.

BREAKFAST.—Boiled Weak Fish, Beefsteak, Head Cheese, Sausage, Omelet.
DINNER.—Oysters on shell, Onion Soup, Kidney Pie, White Fish, Chicken, Succory Salad, American Cream Cheese, Mince Meat Pie.
SUPPER.—Wild Ducks, Smoked Beef Tongue, Chicken Salad, Roquefort Cheese, Sliced Oranges and Cake.

FRIDAY 25th.

BREAKFAST.—Fish Croquettes, Brook Trout, Boned Herrings and Fried Eggs.
DINNER.—Oyster Stew, Devilled Crabs, Cured Cod Fish, Cole Slaw, Neufchatel Cheese, Apple Dumplings.
SUPPER.—Clam Fritters, Macaroni, Eggs on Toast, Herring Salad, Gruyere Cheese, Roasted Chestnuts, Blackberry Jelly and Cake.

SATURDAY 26th.

BREAKFAST.—Fresh Herrings, Broiled Veal Cutlets, Quails, Omelet.
DINNER.—Julienne Soup, Oyster Patties, Sheep's Head Fish, Beef a la mode, Corn Salad, Cheese Pie.
SUPPER.—Meat Croquettes, Pickled Mackerel, Potato Salad, Camembert Cheese, Apple Jelly and Cake.

SUNDAY 27th.

BREAKFAST.—Shrimps Patties, Liver and Bacon, Sweet-breads, Eggs.
DINNER.—Oysters on shell, Beef Soup, Vole-au-vent, Fresh Salmon, Turkey, Lettuce Salad, Plum Pudding, Roquefort Cheese, Ice Cream.
SUPPER.—Chicken Croquettes, Meat Jelly, Lobster Salad, Parmesant Cheese, Sliced Oranges and Cake.

JANUARY, MONDAY 28th.

BREAKFAST.—Boiled Fresh Mackerel, Beefsteak, Sausage, Omelet.

DINNER.—Split-Pea Soup, Woodcock Pie, Pike, Fresh Boiled Beef, Cole Slaw, Brie Cheese, Apple Pie.

SUPPER.—Fried Oysters, Head Cheese, Eggs on Toast, Succory Salad, American Cream Cheese, Stoned Cherries and Cake.

TUESDAY 29th.

BREAKFAST.—Yellow Cat Fish, Mutton Chops, Pig's Feet, Ham and Eggs.

DINNER.—Ox-Tail Soup, Snipes, Fresh Cod Fish, Roast Beef, Corn Salad, Gruyere Cheese, Currant Jelly Pie. ·

SUPPER.—Wild Rabbit Pie, Omelet, Celery Salad, Munster Cheese, Cranberry Jelly and Cake.

WEDNESDAY 30th.

BREAKFAST.—Blue Fish, Porksteak, Scrappel, Sausage Pudding, Eggs.

DINNER.—Shelled Bean Soup, Chicken Croquettes, Gray Perch, Leg of Mutton, Turnip Sprouts Salad, Schweizer Cheese, Stoned Cherry Pie.

SUPPER.—Meat Croquettes, Cold Ham, Crab Salad, Emmenthal Cheese, Green Winter Berries and Cake.

THURSDAY 31st.

BREAKFAST.—Boiled Weak Fish, Beefsteak, Sheep's Head, Sausage, Omelet.

DINNER.—Oysters on half shell, Onion Soup, Quails, White Fish, Chicken, Succory Salad, American Cream Cheese, Mince Meat Pie.

SUPPER.—Broiled Porksteak, Chicken Salad, Sardines Roquefort Cheese, Sliced Oranges and Cake.

FEBRUARY.

FRIDAY 1st.

BREAKFAST.—Fish Croquettes, Flounders, Boned Herrings and Fried Eggs.

DINNER.—Oyster Stew, Devilled Crabs, Cured Cod Fish, Cole Slaw, Neufchatel Cheese, Rice Pudding.

SUPPER.—Clam Fritters, Macaroni, Eggs on Toast, Herring Salad, Gruyere Cheese, Roasted Chestnuts, Prunes and Cake.

SATURDAY 2d.

BREAKFAST.—Scallops, Broiled Veal Cutlets, Wild Duck Pie, Omelet.

DINNER.—Julienne Soup, Oyster Patties, Halibut, Roast Veal, Corn Salad, Cheese Pie.

SUPPER.—Meat Croquettes, Pickled Salmon, Potato Salad, Camembert Cheese, Apple Jelly and Cake.

SUNDAY 3d.

BREAKFAST.—Shrimps Patties, Liver and Bacon, Sweet-breads, Eggs.

DINNER.—Oysters on half shell, Beef Soup, Vole-au-vent, Sheep's Head Fish, Canvasback Ducks, Lettuce Salad, Plum Pudding, Roquefort Cheese, Ice Cream.

SUPPER.—Chicken Croquettes, Meat Jelly, Lobster Salad, Parmesant Cheese, Sliced Oranges and Cake.

8

FEBRUARY, MONDAY 4th.

BREAKFAST.—Boiled Fresh Mackerel, Beefsteak, Sausage, Omelet.
DINNER.—Split-Pea Soup, Kidneys, Pike, Corned Beef, Corn Salad, Brie Cheese, Apple Pie.
SUPPER.—Fried Oysters, Calf's Feet, Head Cheese, Anchovy Salad, American Cream Cheese, Stewed Pears and Cake.

TUESDAY 5th.

BREAKFAST.—Boiled Smelts, Mutton Chops, Pig's Livers, Ham and Eggs.
DINNER.—Clam Soup, Oyster Crab Patties, Fresh Cod Fish, Roast Beef, Cole Slaw, Gruyere Cheese, Currant Jelly Pie.
SUPPER.—Mutton Stew, Omelet, Celery Salad, Munster Cheese, Prunes and Cake.

WEDNESDAY 6th.

BREAKFAST.—Blue Fish, Porksteaks, Fresh Beef's Tongue, Eggs.
DINNER.—Shelled-Bean Soup, Chicken Croquettes, Rock Fish, Leg of Mutton, Water Cress Salad, Schweizer Cheese, Cocoanut Pie.
SUPPER.—Meat Croquettes, White Sausage, Fresh Fish Salad, Emmenthal Cheese, Raspberry Jelly and Cake.

THURSDAY 7th.

BREAKFAST.—Weak Fish, Beefsteak, Head Cheese, Sausage, Omelet.
DINNER.—Oysters on shell, Onion Soup, Kidneys Pie, White Fish, Chicken, Succory Salad, American Cream Cheese, Mince Meat Pie.
SUPPER.—Broiled Porksteak, Smoked Beef Tongue, Chicken Salad, Roquefort Cheese, Sliced Oranges and Cake.

FRIDAY 8th.

BREAKFAST.—Fish Croquettes, Blue Fish, Boned Herrings and Fried Eggs.
DINNER.—Oyster Stew, Devilled Crabs, Cured Cod Fish, Cole Slaw, Neufchatel Cheese, Apple Dumplings
SUPPER.—Clam Fritters, Macaroni, Eggs on Toast, Herring Salad, Roasted Chestnuts, Camembert Cheese, Cranberry Jelly and Cake.

SATURDAY 9th.

BREAKFAST.—Fresh Herrings, Broiled Veal Cutlets, Calf's Brains, Omelet.
DINNER.—Julienne Soup, Oyster Patties, Black Bass, Sour Kraut and Pork, Corn Salad, Cheese Pie.
SUPPER.—Meat Croquettes, Pickled Mackerel, Potatoe Salad, Gruyere Cheese, Apple Jelly and Cake.

SUNDAY 10th.

BREAKFAST.—Shrimp Patties, Liver and Bacon, Sweet-breads, Eggs.
DINNER.—Raw Oysters on Half Shell, Beef Soup, Vole-au-vent, Fresh Salmon, Trout, Prarie Chicken, Lettuce, Plum Pudding, Roquefort Cheese, Ice Cream.
SUPPER.—Chicken Croquettes, Meat Jelly, Lobster Salad, Parmesant Cheese, Sliced Oranges and Cake.

FEBRUARY, MONDAY 11th.

BREAKFAST.—Boiled Fresh Mackerel, Beefsteak, Sausage, Omelet.
DINNER.—Split-Pea Soup, Giblet's Pie, Pike, Fresh Boiled Beef, Cole Slaw, Brie
Cheese, Apple Pie.
SUPPER.—Fried Oysters, Kidneys, Head Cheese, String Bean Salad, American Cream
Cheese, Stewed Dry Pears and Cake.

TUESDAY 12th.

BREAKFAST.—Cod Fish Tongues, Mutton Chops, Quails, Ham and Eggs.
DINNER.—Bouille Abaisse, Oyster Crab Patties, Fresh Cod Fish, Roast Beef, Corn
Salad, Gruyere Cheese, Cranberry Pie.
SUPPER.—Calf's Head, White Sausage, Omelet, Turnip Sprouts Salad, Munster Cheese,
Quince Marmalade and Cake.

WEDNESDAY 13th.

BREAKFAST.—Blue Fish, Broiled Porksteak, Calf's Brains, Eggs on Toast.
DINNER.—Shelled Bean Soup, Chicken Croquettes, Rock Fish, Leg of Mutton.
Scorzonera Sprouts Salad, Schweizer Cheese, Custard Pie.
SUPPER.—Meat Croquettes, Calf's Feet, Cold Ham, Crab Salad, Emmenthal Cheese,
Stoned Cherries and Cake.

THURSDAY 14th.

BREAKFAST.—Weak Fish, Beefsteak. Head Cheese, Sausage, Omelet.
DINNER.—Oysters on shell, Onion Soup, Tripe, White Fish, Chicken, Endive Salad,
American Cream Cheese. Mince Meat Pie.
SUPPER.—Broiled Veal Steak, Sardines, Chicken Salad, Roquefort Cheese, Sliced
Oranges and Cake.

FRIDAY 15th.

BREAKFAST.—Fish Croquettes. Flounders, Boned Herrings and Fried Eggs.
DINNER.—Oyster Stew, Devilled Crabs, Cured Cod Fish, Cole Slaw, Neufchatel
Cheese, Rice Pudding.
SUPPER.—Clam Fritters, Macaroni, Eggs on Toast, Herring Salad, Gruyere Cheese,
Roasted Chestnuts, Prunes and Cake.

SATURDAY 16th.

BREAKFAST.—Yellow Cat Fish, Broiled Veal Cutlets, Quails, Omelet.
DINNER.—Julienne Soup, Oyster Patties, Sheep's Head Fish, Roast Lamb, Corn
Salad, Cheese Pie.
SUPPER.—Meat Croquettes, Pickled Salmon, Potato Salad, Camembert Cheese, Stewed
Dry Pears and Cake.

SUNDAY 17th.

BREAKFAST.—Shrimps Patties, Liver and Bacon, Sweet-breads, Eggs.
DINNER.—Raw Oysters on half shell, Beef Soup, Vole-au-vent, Black Bass, Filet of
Beef, Lettuce, Plum Pudding, Roquefort Cheese, Ice Cream.
SUPPER.—Chicken Croquettes, Meat Jelly. Lobster Salad, Parmesant Cheese, Sliced
Oranges and Cake.

FEBRUARY, MONDAY 18th.

BREAKFAST.—Boiled Fresh Mackerel, Beefsteak, Sausage, Omelet.
DINNER.—Split-Pea Soup, Quails, Pike, Fresh Boiled Beef, Cole Slaw, Brie Cheese.
Apple Pie.
SUPPER.—Fried Oysters, Kidneys, Head Cheese, Turnip Sprouts Salad, American
Cheese, Currant Jelly and Cake.

TUESDAY 19th.

BREAKFAST.—Flounders, Mutton Chops, Calf's Brains, Ham and Eggs.
DINNER.—Green Turtle Soup, Calf's Feet, Fresh Cod Fish, Roast Beef, Corn Salad,
Gruyere Cheese, Cranberry Pie.
SUPPER.—Mutton Stew, Omelet, Boiled Beef Salad, Munster Cheese, Green Winter
Berries and Cake.

WEDNESDAY 20th.

BREAKFAST.—Cod Fish Tongues, Broiled Porksteak, Fresh Beef's Tongue, Eggs.
DINNER.—Shelled Bean Soup, Chicken Croquettes, Rock Fish, Leg of Mutton, Water
Cress Salad, Schweizer Cheese, Stoned Cherry Pie.
SUPPER.—Meat Croquettes, Strasburg fat Liver, Fresh Fish Salad, Emmenthal
Cheese, Raspberry Jelly and Cake.

THURSDAY 21st.

BREAKFAST.—Weak Fish, Beefsteak, Head Cheese, Sausage, Omelet.
DINNER.—Oysters on shell, Onion Soup, Wild Duck Pie, Ray, Chicken, Succory
Salad, American Cream Cheese, Mince Meat Pie.
SUPPER.—Broiled Porksteak, Boned Wild Rabbit Pie, Chicken Salad, Roquefort
Cheese, Sliced Oranges and Cake.

FRIDAY 22d.

BREAKFAST.—Fish Croquettes, Blue Fish, Boned Herrings and Fried Eggs.
DINNER.—Oyster Soup, Devilled Crabs, Cured Cod Fish, Cole Slaw, Neufchatel
Cheese, Apple Dumplings.
SUPPER.—Clam Fritters, Macaroni, Eggs on Toast, Herring Salad, Brie Cheese
Roasted Chestnut, Cranberry Jelly and Cake.

SATURDAY 23d.

BREAKFAST.—Yellow Perch, Broiled Veal Cutlets, Pudding Sausage, Omelet.
DINNER.—Julienne Soup, Oyster Patties, Salmon Trout, Roast Pork, Corn Salad,
Cheese Pie.
SUPPER.—Meat Croquettes, Pickled Mackerel, Potato Salad, Camembert Cheese, Apple
Jelly and Cake.

SUNDAY 24th.

BREAKFAST.—Shrimps Patties, Liver and Bacon, Sweet-breads, Eggs
DINNER.—Oysters on shell, Beef Soup, Vole-au-vent, Fresh Salmon, Turkey, Lettuce
Salad, Plum Pudding, Roquefort Cheese, Ice Cream.
SUPPER.—Chicken Croquettes, Meat Jelly, Lobster Salad, Parmesant Cheese, Sliced
Oranges and Cake.

FEBRUARY, MONDAY 25th.

BREAKFAST.—Boiled Fresh Mackerel, Beefsteak, Sausage, Omelet.
DINNER.—Split-Pea Soup, Sheep's Feet, Pike, Fresh Boiled Beef, Cole Slaw, Brie Cheese, Apple Pie.
SUPPER.—Fried Oysters, Kidneys, Head Cheese, Celery Salad, American Cream Cheese, Currant Jelly and Cake.

TUESDAY 26th.

BREAKFAST.—Scallops, Mutton Chops, Warm Pig's Feet, Ham and Eggs.
DINNER.—Green Turtle Soup, Wild Boned Rabbit Pie, Fresh Cod Fish, Roast Beef, Corn Salad, Gruyere Cheese, Cranberry Pie.
SUPPER.—Wild Duck Pie, Calf's Feet, Omelet, Corn Salad, Munster Cheese, Quince Marmalade and Cake.

WEDNESDAY 27th.

BREAKFAST.—Blue Fish, Porksteak, Scrappel, Sausage Pudding, Eggs.
DINNER.—Shelled-Bean Soup, Chicken Croquettes, White Perch, Leg of Mutton, Turnip Sprouts Salad, Schweizer Cheese, Custard Pie.
SUPPER.—Meat Croquettes, Calf's Brains, Cold Ham, Crab Salad, Emmenthal Cheese, Stoned Cherries and Cake.

THURSDAY 28th.

BREAKFAST.—Boiled Weak Fish, Beefsteak, Head Cheese, Sausage, Omelet.
DINNER.—Raw Oysters on half shell, Onion Soup, Tripe, White Fish, Chicken, Red Cabbage Salad, American Cream Cheese, Mince Meat Pie.
SUPPER.—Porksteak, Sardines, Chicken Salad, Roquefort Cheese, Sliced Oranges and Cake.

FRIDAY 29th.

BREAKFAST.—Fish Croquettes, King Fish, Boned Herrings and Fried Eggs
DINNER.—Oyster Soup, Devilled Crabs, Cured Cod Fish, Cole Slaw, Neufchatel Cheese, Rice Pudding.
SUPPER.—Clam Fritters, Macaroni, Eggs on Toast, Herring Salad, Gruyere Cheese, Roasted Chestnuts, Prunes and Cake.

MARCH.

SATURDAY 1st.

BREAKFAST.—Smelts, Broiled Veal Cutlets, Kidneys, Omelet.
DINNER.—Julienne Soup, Oyster Patties, Haddock, Beef-a-la-mode, Corn Salad, Cheese Pie.
SUPPER.—Meat Croquettes, Pickled Salmon, Potatoe Salad, Camembert Cheese, Stewed Dry Pears and Cake.

SUNDAY 2d.

BREAKFAST.—Shrimp Patties, Liver and Bacon, Sweet-breads, Eggs.
DINNER.—Oysters on shell, Beef Soup, Vole-au-vent, Sheep's Head Fish, Canvas-back Duck, Lettuce Salad, Roquefort Cheese, Plum Pudding, Ice Cream.
SUPPER.—Chicken Croquettes, Meat Jelly, Lobster Salad, Parmesant Cheese, Sliced Oranges and Cake.

MARCH, MONDAY 3d.

BREAKFAST.—Boiled Fresh Mackerel, Beefsteak, Sausage, Omelet.

DINNER.—Split-Pea Soup, Sheep's Feet, Pike, Corned Beef, Corn Sa'ad, Brie Cheese, Apple Pie.

SUPPER.—Fried Oysters, Kidneys, Head Cheese, Celery Salad, American Cream Cheese, Stoned Cherries and Cake.

TUESDAY 4th.

BREAKFAST.—Eels, Broiled Mutton Chops, Pig's Liver, Ham and Eggs.

DINNER.—Ox-Tail Soup, Wild Duck Pie, Fresh Cod Fish, Roast Beef, Cole Slaw, Gruyere Cheese, Cranberry Pie.

SUPPER.—Mutton Stew, Calf's Feet, Omelet, Corn Salad, Munster Cheese, Quince Marmalade and Cake.

WEDNESDAY 5th.

BREAKFAST.—Blue Fish, Porksteak, Fresh Beef's Tongue, Eggs on Toast.

DINNER.—Shelled Bean Soup, Chicken Croquettes, Rock Fish, Leg of Mutton, Water Cress Salad, Parmesant Cheese, Cocoanut Pie.

SUPPER.—Meat Croquettes, Warm Pig's Feet, Fresh Fish Salad, Emmenthal Cheese, Stoned Cherries and Cake.

THURSDAY 6th.

BREAKFAST.—Weak Fish, Beefsteak, Head Cheese, Sausage, Omelet.

DINNER.—Raw Oysters on half shell, Onion Soup, Kidney's Pie, White Fish, Chicken, Red Cabbage Salad, American Cream Cheese, Mince Meat Pie.

SUPPER.—Broiled Porksteak, Sardines, Chicken Salad, Roquefort Cheese, Sliced Oranges and Cake.

FRIDAY 7th.

BREAKFAST.—Fish Croquettes, Yellow Perch, Boned Herrings and Fried Eggs.

DINNER.—Oyster Soup, Devilled Crabs, Cured Cod Fish, Cole Slaw, Neufchatel Cheese, Apple Dumplings.

SUPPER.—Clam Fritters, Macaroni, Eggs on Toast, Herring Salad, Brie Cheese, Roasted Chestnuts, Cranberry Jelly and Cake.

SATURDAY 8th,

BREAKFAST.—Flounders, Veal Cutlets, Pudding Sausage, Scrappel, Omelet.

DINNER.—Julienne Soup, Oyster Patties, Sheep's Head Fish, Roast Veal, Corn Salad, Cheese Pie.

SUPPER.—Meat Croquettes, Pickled Mackerel, Potato Salad, Camembert Cheese, Apple Jelly and Cake.

SUNDAY 9th.

BREAKFAST.—Shrimps Patties, Liver and Bacon, Sweet-breads, Eggs.

DINNER.—Oysters on shell, Beef Soup, Vole-au-vent, Fresh Lake Trout, Wild Goose, Lettuce Salad, Roquefort Cheese, Plum Pudding, Ice Cream.

SUPPER.—Chicken Croquettes, Meat Jelly, Lobster Salad, Parmesant Cheese, Sliced Oranges and Cake.

MARCH, MONDAY 10th.

BREAKFAST.—Boiled Fresh Mackerel, Beefsteak, Sausage, Omelet.
DINNER.—Split-Pea Soup, Wild Duck Pie, Pike, Fresh Boiled Beef, Cole Slaw, Brie
Cheese, Apple Pie.
SUPPER.—Fried Oysters, Kidneys, Head Cheese, Red Cabbage Salad, American Cream
Cheese, Stoned Cherries and Cake.

TUESDAY 11th.

BREAKFAST.—Yellow Perch, Mutton Chops, Fresh Beef's Tongues, Ham and Eggs
DINNER.—Turtle Soup, Oyster Crab Patties, Fresh Cod Fish, Roast Beef, Corn
Salad, Gruyere Cheese, Cranberry Pie.
SUPPER.—Calf's Feet, Omelet, White Sausage, Boiled Beef Salad, Munster Cheese,
Prunes and Cake.

WEDNESDAY 12th.

BREAKFAST.—Blue Fish, Broiled Porksteak, Calf's Brains, Eggs on Toast.
DINNER.—Shelled Bean Soup, Chicken Croquettes, Ray, Leg of Mutton, Turnip
Sprouts Salad, Schweizer Cheese, Stoned Cherry Pie.
SUPPER.—Meat Croquettes, Omelet, Cold Ham, Crab Salad, Emmenthal Cheese,
Blackberry Jelly and Cake.

THURSDAY 13th.

BREAKFAST.—Boiled Weak Fish, Beefsteak, Head Cheese, Sausage, Boiled Eggs.
DINNER.—Oysters on shell, Onion Soup, Sheep's Head Fish, Chicken, Corn Salad,
American Cream Cheese, Mince Meat Pie.
SUPPER.—Broiled Porksteak, Sardines, Chicken Salad, Roquefort Cheese, Sliced
Oranges and Cake.

FRIDAY 14th.

BREAKFAST.—Fish Croquettes, King Fish, Boned Herrings and Fried Eggs.
DINNER.—Oyster Stew, Devilled Crabs, Cured Cod Fish, Cole Slaw, Neufchatel
Cheese, Rice Pudding.
SUPPER.—Clam Fritters, Macaroni, Eggs on Toast, Herring Salad, Gruyere Cheese,
Roasted Chestnuts, Prunes and Cake.

SATURDAY 15th.

BREAKFAST.—Cod Fish Tongues, Broiled Veal Cutlets, Scrappel, Omelet.
DINNER.—Julienne Soup, Oyster Patties, Halibut, Sour Kraut and Pork, Corn Salad,
Cheese Pie.
SUPPER.—Meat Croquettes, Pickled Salmon, Potato Salad, Camembert Cheese, Currant
Jelly and Cake.

SUNDAY 16th.

BREAKFAST.—Shrimps Patties, Liver and Bacon, Sweet-breads, Eggs.
DINNER.—Oysters on shell, Beef Soup, Vole-au-vent, Black Bass, Filet of Beef,
Lettuce Salad, Roquefort Cheese, Plum Pudding, Ice Cream.
SUPPER.—Chicken Croquettes, Meat Jelly, Lobster Salad, Parmesant Cheese, Sliced
Oranges and Cake.

MARCH, MONDAY 17th.

BREAKFAST.—Boiled Fresh Mackerel, Beefsteak, Sausage, Omelet.
DINNER.—Split-Pea Soup, Kidneys, Pike, Fresh Boiled Beef, Cole Slaw, Brie Cheese, Apple Pie.
SUPPER.—Fried Oysters, Sheep's Feet, Head Cheese, Anchovy Salad, American Cream Cheese, Currant Jelly and Cake.

TUESDAY 18th.

BREAKFAST.—Boiled King Fish, Mutton Chops, Pig's Liver, Ham and Eggs.
DINNER.—Ox-Tail Soup, Oyster Crab Patties, Fresh Cod Fish, Roast Beef, Corn Salad, Gruyere Cheese, Raspberry Jelly Pie.
SUPPER.—Mutton Stew, Omelet, White Sausage, Celery Salad, Gruyere Cheese, Prunes and Cake.

WEDNESDAY 19th.

BREAKFAST.—Blue Fish, Porksteaks, Fresh Calf's Tongues, Eggs on Toast.
DINNER.—Shelled Bean Soup, Chicken Croquettes, Rock Fish, Leg of Mutton, Water Cress Salad, Schweizer Cheese, Custard Pie.
SUPPER.—Meat Croquettes, Pig's Feet, Fresh Fish Salad, Emmenthal Cheese, Raspberry Jelly and Cake.

THURSDAY 20th.

BREAKFAST.--Boiled Weak Fish, Beefsteak, Head Cheese, Sausage, Omelet.
DINNER.—Oysters on shell, Onion Soup, Wild Duck Pie, White Fish, Chicken Red Cabbage Salad, American Cream Cheese, Mince Meat Pie.
SUPPER.—Broiled Porksteak, Smoked Beef's Tongue, Chicken Salad, Roquefort Cheese, Sliced Oranges and Cake.

FRIDAY 21st.

BREAKFAST.—Fish Croquettes, Flounders, Boned Herrings and Fried Eggs.
DINNER.—Oyster Soup, Devilled Crabs, Cured Cod Fish, Cole Slaw, Neufchatel Cheese, Apple Dumplings.
SUPPER.—Clam Fritters, Macaroni, Eggs on Toast, Herring Salad, Roasted Chestnuts, Camembert Cheese, Cranberry Jelly and Cake.

SATURDAY 22d.

BREAKFAST.—Boiled Yellow Cat Fish, Broiled Veal Cutlets, Pudding Sausage, Omelet.
DINNER.—Julienne Soup, Oyster Patties, Black Bass, Roast Lamb, Corn Salad, Cheese Pie.
SUPPER.—Meat Croquettes, Pickled Mackerel, Potato Salad, Brie Cheese, Apple Jelly and Cake.

SUNDAY 23d.

BREAKFAST.—Shrimps Patties, Liver and Bacon, Sweet-breads, Eggs
DINNER.—Oysters on shell, Beef Soup, Vole-au-vent, Fresh Salmon, Turkey, Lettuce Salad, Plum Pudding, Roquefort Cheese, Ice Cream.
SUPPER.—Chicken Croquettes, Meat Jelly, Lobster Salad, Parmesant Cheese, Sliced Oranges and Cake.

MARCH, MONDAY 24th.

BREAKFAST.—Boiled Fresh Mackerel, Beefsteak, Sausage, Omelet.
DINNER.—Split-Pea Soup, Giblets Pie, Pike, Fresh Boiled Fish, Cole Slaw, Brie
Cheese, Apple Pie.
SUPPER.—Fried Oysters, Kidneys, Head Cheese, Water Cress Salad, American Cream
Cheese, Currant Jelly and Cake.

TUESDAY 25th.

BREAKFAST.—Fresh Herrings, Mutton Chops, Fresh Beef's Tongue, Ham and Eggs.
DINNER.—Turtle Soup, Oyster Crab Patties, Fresh Cod Fish, Roast Beef, Corn Salad,
Gruyere Cheese, Currant Jelly Pie.
SUPPER.—Mutton Stew, Calf's Brains, Omelet, Red Cabbage Salad, Munster Cheese,
Prunes and Cake.

WEDNESDAY 26th.

BREAKFAST.—Blue Fish, Broiled Porksteak, Fresh Calf's Tongue, Eggs.
DINNER.—Shelled Bean Soup, Chicken Croquettes, Rock Fish, Leg of Mutton, Water
Cress Salad, Schweizer Cheese, Custard Pie.
SUPPER.—Meat Croquettes, Pig's Feet, Crab Salad, Emmenthal Cheese, Raspberry
Jelly and Cake.

THURSDAY 27th.

BREAKFAST.—Boiled Weak Fish, Beefsteak. Head Cheese, Sausage, Omelet.
DINNER.—Oysters on shell, Onion Soup, Wild Duck Pie, White Fish, Chicken, Corn
Salad, American Cream Cheese, Mince Meat Pie.
SUPPER.—Broiled Porksteak, Smoked Beef's Tongue, Chicken Salad, Roquefort
Cheese, Sliced Oranges and Cake.

FRIDAY 28th.

BREAKFAST.—Fish Croquettes, Yellow Cat Fish, Boned Herrings and Fried Eggs.
DINNER.—Oyster Soup, Devilled Crabs, Cured Cod Fish, Cole Slaw, Neufchatel
Cheese, Apple Dumplings.
SUPPER.—Clam Fritters, Macaroni, Bull Frog Legs, Herring Salad, Roasted Chest-
nuts, Camembert Cheese, Cranberry Jelly and Cake.

SATURDAY 29th.

BREAKFAST.—Yellow Perch, Broiled Veal Cutlets, Pudding Sausage, Omelet.
DINNER.—Julienne Soup, Oyster Patties, Black Bass, Roast Pork, Corn Salad,
Cheese Pie.
SUPPER.—Meat Croquettes, Pickled Salmon, Potato Salad, Brie Cheese, Apple Jelly
and Cake.

SUNDAY 30th.

BREAKFAST.—Shrimps Patties, Liver and Bacon, Sweet-breads, Eggs.
DINNER.—Oysters on shell, Beef Soup, Vole-au-vent, Fresh Salmon, Chicken, Lettuce
Salad, Plum Pudding, Roquefort Cheese, Ice Cream.
SUPPER.—Chicken Croquettes, Meat Jelly, Lobster Salad, Roquefort Cheese, Sliced
Oranges and Cake.

MARCH, MONDAY 31st.

BREAKFAST.—Boiled Fresh Mackerel, Beefsteak, Sausage, Omelet.
DINNER.—Split-Pea Soup, Kidneys, Pike, Corned Beef, Corn Salad, Brie Cheese, Apple Pie.
SUPPER.—Fried Oysters, Head Cheese, Calf's Feet, String Bean Salad, American Cream Cheese, Prunes and Cake.

APRIL.

TUESDAY 1st.

BREAKFAST.—Flounders, Mutton Chops, Pig's Liver, Ham and Eggs.
DINNER.—Ox-Tail Soup, Fresh Calf's Tongues, Fresh Cod Fish, Cole Slaw, Gruyere Cheese, Currant Jelly Pie.
SUPPER.—Mutton Stew, Omelet, Boiled Beef Salad, Munster Cheese, Cranberry Jelly and Cake.

WEDNESDAY 2d.

BREAKFAST.—Cod Tongues, Broiled Porksteak, Calf's Brains, Eggs on Toast.
DINNER.—Shelled-Bean Soup, Chicken Croquettes, Ray, Leg of Mutton, Dandelion Salad, Schweizer Cheese, Cocoanut Pie.
SUPPER.—Meat Croquettes, Sheep's Feet, Fresh Fish Salad, Emmenthal Cheese, Raspberry Jelly and Cake.

THURSDAY 3d.

BREAKFAST.—Weak Fish, Beefsteak, Head Cheese, Sausage, Omelet
DINNER.—Oysters on shell, Onion Soup, Oyster Crab Patties, White Fish, Chicken, Corn Salad, American Cream Cheese, Stoned Cherry Pie.
SUPPER.—Veal Stew, Smoked Beef's Tongues, Chicken Salad, Roquefort Cheese, Sliced Oranges and Cake.

FRIDAY 4th.

BREAKFAST.—Fish Croquettes, Yellow Perch, Boned Herrings and Fried Eggs
DINNER.—Oyster Soup, Devilled Crabs, Cured Cod Fish, Cole Slaw, Neufchatel Cheese, Apple Dumplings.
SUPPER.—Clam Fritters, Macaroni, Eggs on Toast, Herring Salad, Camembert Cheese, Cranberry Jelly and Cake.

SATURDAY 5th.

BREAKFAST.—Fresh Herrings, Veal Cutlets, Scrappel, Pudding Sausage, Omelet.
DINNER.—Julienne Soup, Oyster Patties, Black Bass, Beef-a-la-mode, Corn Salad, Cheese Pie.
SUPPER.—Meat Croquettes, Pickled Mackerel, Potatoe Salad, Munster Cheese, Apple Jelly and Cake.

SUNDAY 6th.

BREAKFAST.—Shrimp Patties, Liver and Bacon, Sweet-breads, Eggs.
DINNER.—Raw Oysters on shell, Beef Soup, Vole-au-vent, Salmon Trout, Sucking Pig, Lettuce Salad, Roquefort Cheese, Plum Pudding, Ice Cream.
SUPPER.—Chicken Croquettes, Meat Jelly, Lobster Salad, Parmesant Cheese, Sliced Oranges and Cake.

APRIL, MONDAY 7th.

BREAKFAST.—Boiled Fresh Mackerel, Beefsteak, Sausage, Omelet.
DINNER.—Split-Pea Soup, Sheep's Feet, Pike, Fresh Boiled Beef, Cole Slaw, Brie Cheese, Apple Pie.
SUPPER.—Fried Oysters, Kidneys, Head Cheese, Turnip Sprouts Salad, American Cream Cheese, Currant Jelly and Cake.

TUESDAY 8th.

BREAKFAST.—Brook Trout, Mutton Chops, Fresh Beef's Tongues, Ham and Eggs.
DINNER.—Clam Soup, Strasburg Fat Liver, Fresh Cod Fish, Roast Beef, Corn Salad, Gruyere Cheese, Cranberry Pie.
SUPPER.—Wild Duck Pie, Calf's Brains, Omelet, Oyster Crab Salad, Munster Cheese, Quince Marmalade and Cake.

WEDNESDAY 9th.

BREAKFAST.—Blue Fish, Broiled Porksteak, Pig's Feet, Eggs on Toast.
DINNER.—Shelled Bean Soup, Chicken Croquettes, Rock Fish, Leg of Mutton, Dandelion Salad, Schweizer Cheese, Stoned Cherry Pie.
SUPPER.—Meat Croquettes, Calf's Feet, Cold Ham, Crab Salad, Emmenthal Cheese, Prunes and Cake.

THURSDAY 10th.

BREAKFAST.—Boiled Weak Fish, Beefsteak, Head Cheese. Sausage, Boiled Eggs.
DINNER.—Oysters on shell, Onion Soup, Tripe, White Fish, Chicken, String Bean Salad, Parmesant Cheese, Mince Meat Pie.
SUPPER.—Veal Stew, Sardines, Chicken Salad, Roquefort Cheese, Sliced Oranges and Cake.

FRIDAY 11th.

BREAKFAST.—Fish Croquettes, Sheep's Head Fish, Boned Herrings and Fried Eggs.
DINNER.—Oyster Stew, Deviled Crabs, Cured Cod Fish, Cole Slaw, Neufchatel Cheese, Rice Pudding.
SUPPER.—Clam Fritters, Macaroni, Eggs on Toast, Herring Salad, Camembert Cheese, Cranberry Jelly and Cake.

SATURDAY 12th.

BREAKFAST.—Flounders, Broiled Veal Cutlets. Scrappel, Omelet.
DINNER.—Julienne Soup, Oyster Patties, Sheep's Head Fish, Roast Veal, Corn Salad, Cheese Pie.
SUPPER.—Meat Croquettes, Pickled Salmon, Potato Salad, Munster Cheese, Apple Jelly and Cake.

SUNDAY 13th.

BREAKFAST.—Shrimps Patties, Liver and Bacon, Sweet-breads, Eggs.
DINNER.—Oysters on shell, Beef Soup, Vole-au-vent, Black Bass, Turkey, Lettuce Salad, Roquefort Cheese, Plum Pudding, Ice Cream.
SUPPER.—Chicken Croquettes, Meat Jelly, Lobster Salad, Parmesant Cheese, Sliced Oranges and Cake.

APRIL, MONDAY 14th.

BREAKFAST.—Boiled Fresh Mackerel, Beefsteak, Sausage. Omelet.
DINNER.—Split-Pea Soup, Kidneys, Pike, Fresh Boiled Beef, Cole Slaw, Brie Cheese. Apple Pie.
SUPPER.—Fried Oysters, Sheep's Feet, Head Cheese, Anchovy Salad, American Cream Cheese, Currant Jelly and Cake.

TUESDAY 15th.

BREAKFAST.—Shad. Mutton Chops, Fresh Calf's Tongues, Ham and Eggs.
DINNER.—Ox-Tail Soup, Sweet Bread Patties, Fresh Cod Fish, Roast Beef, Corn Salad, Gruyere Cheese, Raspberry Jelly Pie.
SUPPER.—Mutton Stew, Omelet, Boiled Beef Salad, Munster Cheese, Prunes and Cake.

WEDNESDAY 16th.

BREAKFAST.—Blue Fish. Broiled Porksteaks, Pig's Liver, Eggs on Toast.
DINNER.—Shelled Bean Soup, Chicken Croquettes, Rock Fish, Leg of Mutton, Dandelion Salad, Schweizer Cheese, Custard Pie.
SUPPER.—Meat Croquettes, White Sausage, Fresh Fish Salad, Emmenthal Cheese, Quince Marmalade and Cake.

THURSDAY 17th.

BREAKFAST.—Weak Fish, Beefsteak, Head Cheese, Sausage, Boiled Eggs.
DINNER.—Oysters on shell, Onion Soup, Oyster Crab Patties, Shad, Chicken, String Bean Salad, American Cream Cheese. Mince Meat Pie.
SUPPER.—Veal Stew, Omelet. Smoked Beef's Tongue, Chicken Salad, Roquefort Cheese, Sliced Oranges and Cake.

FRIDAY 18th.

BREAKFAST.—Fish Croquettes, Yellow Perch, Boned Herrings and Fried Eggs.
DINNER.—Oyster Soup, Devilled Crabs, Ray, Cole Slaw, Neufchatel Cheese, Apple Dumplings.
SUPPER.—Clam Fritters, Macaroni, Eggs on Toast, Herring Salad, Munster Cheese, Blackberry Jelly and Cake.

SATURDAY 19th.

BREAKFAST.—Shad, Broiled Veal Cutlets, Pudding Sausage, Omelet.
DINNER.—Julienne Soup, Oyster Patties, Halibut, Sour Kraut and Pork, Corn Salad, Cheese Pie.
SUPPER.—Meat Croquettes, Pickled Mackerel, Potato Salad, Camembert Cheese, Apple Jelly and Cake.

SUNDAY 20th.

BREAKFAST.—Shrimps Patties, Liver and Bacon, Sweet-breads, Eggs
DINNER.—Oysters on shell, Beef Soup, Vole-au-vent, Fresh Salmon, Filet of Beef, Lettuce Salad, Plum Pudding, Roquefort Cheese, Ice Cream.
SUPPER.—Chicken Croquettes, Meat Jelly, Lobster Salad, Parmesant Cheese, Sliced Oranges and Cake.

APRIL, MONDAY 21st.

BREAKFAST.—Boiled Fresh Mackerel, Beefsteak, Sausage, Omelet.
DINNER.—Split-Pea Soup, Calf's Brains, Pike, Fresh Boiled Fish, Cole Slaw, Brie Cheese, Apple Pie.
SUPPER.—Fried Oysters, Calf's Feet, Turnip Sprouts Salad, American Cream Cheese, Currant Jelly and Cake.

TUESDAY 22d.

BREAKFAST.—Shad, Mutton Chops, Fresh Beef's Tongue, Ham and Eggs.
DINNER.—Clam Soup, Wild Duck Pie, Fresh Cod Fish, Roast Beef, Corn Salad, Gruyere Cheese, Rhubarb Pie.
SUPPER.—Calf's Head, Omelet, Warm Pig's Feet, Red Cabbage Salad, Munster Cheese, Prunes and Cake.

WEDNESDAY 23d.

BREAKFAST.—Blue Fish, Broiled Porksteak, Pig's Livers, Eggs on Toast.
DINNER.—Shelled Bean Soup, Chicken Croquettes, Shad, Leg of Mutton, Dandelion Salad, Schweizer Cheese, Stoned Cherry Pie.
SUPPER.—Meat Croquettes, Kidneys, Crab Salad, Emmenthal Cheese, Raspberry Jelly and Cake.

THURSDAY 24th.

BREAKFAST.—Weak Fish, Beefsteak. Head Cheese, Sausage, Omelet.
DINNER.—Oysters on shell, Onion Soup, Tripe, White Fish, Chicken, String Bean Salad, American Cream Cheese, Mince Meat Pie.
SUPPER.—Veal Stew, Sardines, Chicken Salad, Roquefort Cheese, Sliced Oranges and Cake.

FRIDAY 25th.

BREAKFAST.—Fish Croquettes, Shad, Boned Herrings and Fried Eggs.
DINNER.—Oyster Stew, Devilled Crabs, Cured Cod Fish, Cole Slaw, Neufchatel Cheese, Rice Pudding.
SUPPER.—Clam Fritters, Macaroni, Eggs on Toast, Herring Salad, Camembert Cheese, Cranberry Jelly and Cake.

SATURDAY 26th.

BREAKFAST.—Cod Tongues, Broiled Veal Cutlets, Scrappel, Omelet.
DINNER.—Julienne Soup, Oyster Patties, Shad, Roast Lamb, Corn Salad, Cheese Pie.
SUPPER.—Meat Croquettes, Pickled Salmon, Potato Salad, Gruyere Cheese, Apple Jelly and Cake.

SUNDAY 27th.

BREAKFAST.—Shrimps Patties, Liver and Bacon, Sweet-breads, Eggs.
DINNER.—Oysters on shell, Beef Soup, Vole-au-vent, Sheep's Head Fish, Canvas-back Duck, Lettuce Salad, Roquefort Cheese, Plum Pudding, Ice Cream.
SUPPER.—Chicken Croquettes, Meat Jelly, Lobster Salad, Roquefort Cheese, Sliced Oranges and Cake.

APRIL, MONDAY 28th.

BREAKFAST.—Boiled Fresh Mackerel, Beefsteak, Sausage, Omelet.
DINNER.—Split-Pea Soup, Kidneys, Pike, Fresh Boiled Beef, Cole Slaw, Brie Cheese, Apple Pie.
SUPPER.—Fried Oysters, Sheep's Feet, Head Cheese. String Bean Salad, American Cream Cheese, Currant Jelly and Cake.

TUESDAY 29th.

BREAKFAST.—Shad, Mutton Chops, Fresh Calf's Tongues, Ham and Eggs.
DINNER.—Ox-Tail Soup, Sweet-breads Patties, Fresh Cod Fish, Roast Beef, Corn Salad, Gruyere Cheese, Green Currant Pie.
SUPPER.—Mutton Stew, Omelet, Boiled Beef Salad, Munster Cheese, Prunes and Cake.

WEDNESDAY 30th.

BREAKFAST.—Blue Fish, Broiled Porksteak, Pig's Liver, Eggs on Toast.
DINNER.—Shelled-Bean Soup, Chicken Croquettes, White Fish, Leg of Mutton, Dandelion Salad, Schweizer Cheese, Cocoanut Pie.
SUPPER.—Meat Croquettes, Giblet's Pie, Fresh Fish Salad, Emmenthal Cheese, Raspberry Jelly and Cake.

MAY.

THURSDAY 1st.

BREAKFAST.—Weak Fish, Beefsteak, Head Cheese, Sausage, Boiled Eggs.
DINNER.—Oysters on shell, Onion Soup, Oyster Crab Patties, Shad, Chicken, String Bean Salad, American Cream Cheese, Stoned Cherry Pie.
SUPPER.—Veal Stew, Omelet, Smoked Beef's Tongues, Chicken Salad, Roquefort Cheese, Sliced Oranges and Cake.

FRIDAY 2d.

BREAKFAST.—Fish Croquettes, Yellow Cat Fish, Boned Herrings and Fried Eggs.
DINNER.—Oyster Soup, Devilled Crabs, Cured Cod Fish, Cole Slaw, Neufchatel Cheese, Apple Dumplings.
SUPPER.—Clam Fritters, Macaroni, Eggs on Toast, Herring Salad, Camembert Cheese, Apple Jelly and Cake.

SATURDAY 3d.

BREAKFAST.—Shad, Veal Cutlets, Scrappel, Pudding Sausage, Omelet.
DINNER.—Veal Soup, Oyster Patties, Fresh Salmon, Roast Pork, Corn Salad, Cheese Pie.
SUPPER.—Meat Croquettes, Pickled Mackerel, Potato Salad, Camembert Cheese, Apple Jelly and Cake.

SUNDAY 5th.

BREAKFAST.—Shrimp Patties, Liver and Bacon, Sweet-breads, Eggs.
DINNER.—Oysters on shell, Beef Soup, Vole-au-vent. Fresh Lake Trout, Chicken, Lettuce Salad, Roquefort Cheese, Plum Pudding, Ice Cream.
SUPPER.—Chicken Croquettes, Meat Jelly, Lobster Salad, Parmesant Cheese, **Sliced** Oranges and Cake.

MAY, MONDAY 5th.

BREAKFAST.—Boiled Fresh Mackerel, Beefsteak, Sausage, Omelet.
DINNER.—Split-Pea Soup, Calf's Head, Pike, Corned Beef, Corn Salad, Brie Cheese, Apple Pie.
SUPPER.—Veal Cutlets, Head Cheese, Sheep's Feet, Eggs on Toast, Water Cress Salad, American Cream Cheese, Currant Jelly and Cake.

TUESDAY 6th.

BREAKFAST.—Shad, Mutton Chops. Fresh Beef's Tongues, Boiled Eggs.
DINNER.—Clam Soup, Small Oyster Crab Patties, Roast Beef, Cole Slaw, Gruyere Cheese, Raspberry Jelly Pie.
SUPPER.—Warm Pig's Feet, Omelet, Tripe, White Sausage, Pepper Cress Salad, Munster Cheese, Prunes and Cake.

WEDNESDAY 7th.

BREAKFAST.—Blue Fish, Porksteak, Dried Beef, Ham and Eggs.
DINNER.—Shelled Bean Soup, Chicken Croquettes, Salmon Trout, Leg of Mutton, Dandelion Salad, Schweizer Cheese, Strawberry Short Cake.
SUPPER.—Meat Croquettes, Fresh Calf's Tongues, Omelet, Corn Salad, Emmenthal Cheese, Sliced Oranges and Cake.

THURSDAY 8th.

BREAKFAST.—Boiled Weak Fish, Beefsteak, Calf's Brains, Boiled Eggs.
DINNER.—Little Neck Clams on shell, Onion Soup, Sweet Bread Patties, Shad, Chicken, Mixed Salad, American Cream Cheese, Mince Meat Pie.
SUPPER.—Veal Stew, Sardines, Chicken Salad, Roquefort Cheese, Strawberries and Cake.

FRIDAY 9th.

BREAKFAST.—Fish Croquettes, Flounders, Boned Herrings and Fried Eggs.
DINNER.—Oyster Soup, Devilled Crabs, Cured Cod Fish, Cole Slaw, Neufchatel Cheese, Rice Pudding.
SUPPER.—Clam Fritters, Macaroni, Eggs on Toast, Herring Salad, Camembert Cheese, Cranberry Jelly and Cake.

SATURDAY 10th.

BREAKFAST.—Shad, Broiled Veal Cutlets. Fresh Calf's Tongues, Omelet.
DINNER.—Julienne Soup, Calf's Feet, Sheep's Head Fish, Beef-a-la-mode, Corn Salad, Cheese Pie.
SUPPER.—Meat Croquettes, Pickled Salmon, Potato Salad, Gruyere Cheese, Strawberries and Cake.

SUNDAY 11th.

BREAKFAST.—Shrimps Patties, Liver and Bacon, Sweet-breads, Eggs.
DINNER.—Little Neck Clams on shell, Beef Soup, Vole-au-vent, Black Bass, Filet of Beef, Lettuce Salad, Plum Pudding, Roquefort Cheese, Ice Cream.
SUPPER.—Chicken Croquettes, Meat Jelly, Lobster Salad, Parmesant Cheese, Sliced Oranges and Cake.

MAY, MONDAY 12th.

BREAKFAST.—Boiled Fresh Mackerel, Beefsteak, Kidneys, Omelet.
DINNER.—Split-Pea Soup, Calf's Feet, Pike, Fresh Boiled Beef, Cole Slaw, Brie Cheese, Apple Pie.
SUPPER.—Broiled Veal Cutlets, Bacon and Eggs, Anchovy Salad, American Cream Cheese, Strawberries and Cake.

TUESDAY 13th.

BREAKFAST.—Shad, Mutton Chops, Tripe, Eggs on Toast.
DINNER.—Pepper Pot, Oyster Crab Patties, Fresh Cod Fish, Roast Beef. Corn Salad, Gruyere Cheese, Strawberry Short Cake.
SUPPER.—Mutton Stew, Omelet, Boiled Beef Salad, Munster Cheese, Rhubarb with Gooseberries and Cake.

WEDNESDAY 14th.

BREAKFAST.—Blue Fish, Veal Stew, Dried Beef, Ham and Eggs.
DINNER.—Shelled Bean Soup, Chicken Croquettes, Rock Fish, Leg of Mutton, Mixed Salad, Schweizer Cheese, Stoned Cherry Pie.
SUPPER.—Meat Croquettes, Sheep's Feet, Fresh Fish Salad, Emmenthal Cheese, Strawberries and Cake.

THURSDAY 15th.

BREAKFAST.—Boiled Weak Fish, Beefsteak, Fresh Calf's Tongues, Omelet.
DINNER.—Little Neck Clams, Onion Soup, Sweet-bread Patties, Shad, Chicken, Lettuce Salad, American Cream Cheese, Strawberry Short Cake.
SUPPER.—Calf's Head, Smoked Beef's Tongue, Chicken Salad, Roquefort Cheese, Sliced Oranges and Cake.

FRIDAY 16th.

BREAKFAST.—Fish Croquettes, Gudgeons, Boned Herrings and Fried Eggs.
DINNER.—Bouille-a-Baisse, Devilled Crabs, Cured Cod Fish, Cole Slaw, Neufchatel Cheese, Apple Dumplings.
SUPPER.—Clam Fritters, Macaroni, Cod Fish Tongues, Eggs on Toast, Herring Salad, Camembert Cheese, Strawberries and Cake.

SATURDAY 17th.

BREAKFAST.—Shad, Broiled Veal Cutlets, Calf's Brains, Omelet.
DINNER.—Julienne Soup, Fresh Beef's Tongue, Haddock, Roast Veal, Corn Salad, Cheese Pie.
SUPPER.—Meat Croquettes, Pickled Mackerel, Potato Salad, Gruyere Cheese, Strawberries and Cake.

SUNDAY 18th.

BREAKFAST.—Shrimps Patties, Liver and Bacon, Sweet-breads, Eggs
DINNER.—Little Neck Clams, Beef Soup, Vole-au-vent, Fresh Salmon, Canvas-back Duck, Lettuce Salad, Roquefort Cheese, Plum Pudding, Ice Cream.
SUPPER.—Chicken Croquettes, Meat Jelly, Lobster Salad, Parmesant Cheese, Sliced Pine Apple and Cake.

MAY, MONDAY 19;h.

BREAKFAST.—Boiled Fresh Mackerel, Beefsteak, Kidneys, Omelet.
DINNER.—Split-Pea Soup, Giblet's Pie, Pike, Fresh Boiled Fish, Cole Slaw, Brie
Cheese, Strawberry Short Cake.
SUPPER.—Broiled Veal Cutlets, Calf's Feet, String Bean Salad, American Cream
Cheese, Rhubarb with Green Gooseberries and Cake.

TUESDAY 20th.

BREAKFAST.—Shad, Mutton Chops, Tripe, Eggs on Toast.
DINNER.—Ox-Tail Soup, Strasburg's Fat Liver, Fresh Cod Fish, Roast Beef, Corn
Salad, Gruyere Cheese, Green Currant Pie.
SUPPER.—Mutton Stew, Omelet, Pepper Cress Salad, Munster Cheese, Strawberries
and Cake.

WEDNESDAY 21st.

BREAKFAST.—Blue Fish, Dried Beef, Calf's Brains, Ham and Eggs.
DINNER.—Shelled Bean Soup, Chicken Croquettes, Gray Perch, Leg of Mutton,
Mixed Salad, Schweizer Cheese, Apple Pie.
SUPPER.—Meat Croquettes, Eggs on Toast, Sardines, Crab Salad, Emmenthal Cheese,
Strawberries and Cake.

THURSDAY 22d.

BREAKFAST.—Boiled Weak Fish, Beefsteak Sweet-bread Patties, Omelet.
DINNER.—Little Neck Clams, Onion Soup, Tripe, Shad, Chicken, Lettuce Salad,
American Cream Cheese, Strawberry Short Cake.
SUPPER.—Veal Stew, Sheep's Feet, Chicken Salad, Roquefort Cheese, Sliced Oranges
and Cake.

FRIDAY 23d.

BREAKFAST.—Fish Croquettes, Yellow Perch, Boned Herrings and Fried Eggs.
DINNER.—Clam Soup, Devilled Crabs, Cured Cod Fish, Cole Slaw, Neufchatel
Cheese, Rice Pudding.
SUPPER.—Cod Tongue Fritters Macaroni, Eggs on Toast, Herring Salad, Camembert
Cheese, Strawberries and Cake.

SATURDAY 24th.

BREAKFAST.—Shad, Veal Cutlets, Fresh Beef's Tongue, Omelet.
DINNER.—Julienne Soup, Calf's Feet, Black Bass, Sour Kraut and Pork, Mixed Salad,
Cheese Pie.
SUPPER.—Meat Croquettes, Pickled Salmon, Potato Salad, Gruyere Cheese, Straw-
berries and Cake.

SUNDAY 25th.

BREAKFAST.—Shrimps Patties, Liver and Bacon, Sweet-breads, Eggs.
DINNER.—Little Neck Clams, Beef Soup, Vole-au-vent, Sheep's Head, Filet of Beef,
Lettuce Salad, Roquefort Cheese, Plum Pudding, Ice Cream.
SUPPER.—Chicken Croquettes, Meat Jelly, Lobster Salad, Roquefort Cheese, Sliced
Pine Apple and Cake.

MAY, MONDAY 26th.

BREAKFAST.—Boiled Fresh Mackerel, Beefsteak, Kidney, Omelet.
DINNER.—Split-Pea Soup, Calf's Head, Pike, Fresh Boiled Beef, Water Cress Salad, Brie Cheese, Apple Pie.
SUPPER.—Veal Cutlets, Tripe, Eggs on Toast, Cold Ham, Mixed Salad, American Cream Cheese, Strawberries and Cake.

TUESDAY 27th.

BREAKFAST.—Shad, Mutton Chops, Fresh Calf's Tongues, Boiled Eggs.
DINNER.—Ox-Tail Soup, Oyster Crab Patties, Fresh Cod Fish, Roast Beef, Lettuce Salad, Gruyere Cheese, Green Gooseberry Pie.
SUPPER.—Mutton Stew, Omelet, Boiled Beef Salad, Munster Cheese, Strawberries and Cake.

WEDNESDAY 28th.

BREAKFAST.—Blue Fish, Broiled Veal Cutlets, Calf's Brains, Ham and Eggs.
DINNER.—Shelled-Bean Soup, Chicken Croquettes, White Fish, Leg of Mutton, String Bean Salad, Schweizer Cheese, Custard Pie.
SUPPER.—Meat Croquettes, Pig's Feet, Fresh Fish Salad, Emmenthal Cheese, Strawberries and Cake.

THURSDAY 29th.

BREAKFAST.—Boiled Weak Fish, Beefsteak, Sheep's Feet, Omelet.
DINNER.—Little Neck Clams, Onion Soup, Sweet-bread Patties, Shad, Chicken, Lettuce Salad, American Cream Cheese, Strawberry Short Cake.
SUPPER.—Veal Stew, Fresh Beef's Tongues, Chicken Salad, Roquefort Cheese, Sliced Oranges and Cake.

FRIDAY 30th.

BREAKFAST.—Fish Croquettes, Smelts, Boned Herrings and Fried Eggs.
DINNER.—Turtle Soup, Devilled Crabs, Cured Cod Fish, Pepper Cresss Salad, Neufchatel Cheese, Apple Dumplings.
SUPPER.—Clam Fritters, Macaroni, Eggs on Toast, Herring Salad, Camembert Cheese, Strawberries and Cake.

SATURDAY 31st.

BREAKFAST.—Shad, Broiled Veal Cutlets, Ham and Eggs.
DINNER.—Julienne Soup, Calf's Feet, Halibut, Roast Lamb, Mixed Salad, Cheese Pie.
SUPPER.—Meat Croquettes, Pickled Mackerel, Potato Salad, Gruyere Cheese, Strawberries and Cake.

JUNE.

SUNDAY 1st.

BREAKFAST.—Shrimp Patties, Liver and Bacon, Sweet-breads, Eggs.
DINNER.—Little Neck Clams, Beef Soup, Vole-au-vent, Fresh Lake Trout, Chicken, Lettuce Salad, Roquefort Cheese, Plum Pudding, Ice Cream.
SUPPER.—Chicken Croquettes, Meat Jelly, Lobster Salad, Parmesant Cheese, Sliced Pine Apple and Cake.

JUNE, MONDAY 2d.

BREAKFAST.—Boiled Fresh Mackerel, Beefsteak, Kidneys, Omelet.
DINNER.—Split-Pea Soup, Sheep's Feet, Pike, Corned Beef, Water Cress Salad, Brie Cheese, Apple Pie.
SUPPER.—Veal Cutlets, Fresh Beef's Tongue, Cold Ham, String Bean Salad, American Cream Cheese, Strawberries and Cake.

TUESDAY 3d.

BREAKFAST.—Shad, Mutton Chops, Dried Beef, Eggs on Toast.
DINNER.—Clam Chowder, Snails or Tripe, Roast Beef, Lettuce Salad, Gruyere Cheese, Rhubarb Pie.
SUPPER.—Terrapine, Omelet, Boiled Beef Salad, Munster Cheese, Strawberries and Cake.

WEDNESDAY 4th.

BREAKFAST.—Blue Fish, Veal Stew, Ham and Eggs.
DINNER.—Shelled Bean Soup, Chicken Croquettes, Flounders, Leg of Mutton, Water Cress Salad, Schweizer Cheese, Mince Meat Pie.
SUPPER.—Meat Croquettes, Pig's Feet, Sardines, Potato Salad, Emmenthal Cheese, Strawberries and Cake.

THURSDAY 5th.

BREAKFAST.—Boiled Weak Fish, Beefsteak, Calf's Brains, Omelet.
DINNER.—Little Neck Clams, Onion Soup, Sweet Bread Patties, Shad, Chicken, Lettuce Salad, American Cream Cheese, Strawberry Short Cake.
SUPPER.—Veal Stew, Omelet, Chicken Salad, Roquefort Cheese, Sliced Oranges and Cake.

FRIDAY 6th.

BREAKFAST.—Fish Croquettes, Flounders, Boned Herrings and Fried Eggs.
DINNER.—Bouille-a-Baisse Devilled Crabs, Cured Cod Fish, Lettuce Salad, Neufchatel Cheese, Rice Pudding.
SUPPER.—Clam Fritters, Macaroni, Eggs on Toast, Herring Salad, Camembert Cheese, Strawberries and Cake.

SATURDAY 7th.

BREAKFAST.—Shad, Broiled Veal Cutlets, Calf's Feet, Omelet.
DINNER.—Julienne Soup, Young Rabbit Pie, Sheep's Head Fish, Roast Veal, Mixed Salad, Cheese Pie.
SUPPER.—Meat Croquettes, Pickled Salmon, Potato Salad, Gruyere Cheese, Strawberries and Cake.

SUNDAY 8th.

BREAKFAST.—Shrimps Patties, Liver and Bacon, Sweet-breads, Eggs.
DINNER.—Little Neck Clams, Beef Soup, Vole-au-vent, Black Bass, Young Ducks, Cos Salad, Roquefort Cheese, Plum Pudding, Ice Cream.
SUPPER.—Chicken Croquettes, Meat Jelly, Lobster Salad, Parmesant Cheese, Sliced Pine Apple and Cake.

JUNE, MONDAY 9th.

BREAKFAST.—Boiled Fresh Mackerel, Beefsteak, Kidneys, Omelet.
DINNER.—Split-Pea Soup, Calf's Head, Pike, Fresh Boiled Beef, Pepper Cress Salad, Brie Cheese Apple Pie.
SUPPER.—Veal Cutlets, Bacon and Eggs, Anchovy Salad, American Cream Cheese, Strawberries and Cake.

TUESDAY 10th.

BREAKFAST.—Shad, Mutton Chops, Fresh Calf's Tongues, Eggs on Toast
DINNER.—Pepper Pot, Oyster Crab Patties, Fresh Cod Fish, Roast Beef, Lettuce Salad, Gruyere Cheese, Green Gooseberry Pie.
SUPPER.—Mutton Stew, Calf's Feet, Omelet, Cold Smoked Tongue, Mixed Salad, Munster Cheese, Strawberries and Cake.

WEDNESDAY 11th.

BREAKFAST.—Blue Fish, Dried Beef, Calf's Brains, Ham and Eggs.
DINNER.—Shelled Bean Soup, Chicken Croquettes, Rock Fish, Leg of Mutton, Cole Slaw, Schweizer Cheese, Stoned Cherry Pie.
SUPPER.—Meat Croquettes, Giblet's Pie, Fresh Fish Salad, Emmenthal Cheese, Strawberries and Cake.

THURSDAY 12th.

BREAKFAST.—Boiled Weak Fish, Beefsteak, Sheep's Feet, Omelet.
DINNER.—Little Neck Clams, Onion Soup, Sweet-bread Patties, Shad, Chicken. Lettuce Salad, American Cream Cheese, Strawberry Short Cake.
SUPPER.—Veal Stew, Cold Ham, Chicken Salad, Roquefort Cheese, Sliced Oranges and Cake.

FRIDAY 13th.

BREAKFAST.—Fish Croquettes, Yellow Perch, Boned Herrings and Fried Eggs.
DINNER.—Clam Soup, Devilled Crabs, Cured Cod Fish, String Bean Salad, Neufchatel Cheese, Apple Dumplings.
SUPPER.—Cod Tongue Fritters, Macaroni, Eggs on Toast, Herring Salad, Camembert Cheese, Strawberries and Cake.

SATURDAY 14th.

BREAKFAST.—Shad, Broiled Veal Cutlets, Tripe, Omelet.
DINNER.—Julienne Soup, Fresh Beef's Tongue, Lake Trout, Beef-a-la-mode, Lettuce Salad, Cheese Pie.
SUPPER.—Meat Croquettes, Pickled Mackerel, Potato Salad, Muneter Cheese, Strawberries and Cake.

SUNDAY 15th.

BREAKFAST.—Shrimps Patties, Liver and Bacon, Sweet-breads, Eggs
DINNER.—Little Neck Clams, Beef Soup, Vole-au-vent, Fresh Salmon, Filet of Beef, Cos Salad, Roquefort Cheese, Plum Pudding, Ice Cream.
SUPPER.—Chicken Croquettes, Meat Jelly, Lobster Salad, Parmesant Cheese, Sliced Pine Apple and Cake.

JUNE, MONDAY 16th.

BREAKFAST.—Boiled Fresh Mackerel, Beefsteak, Kidneys, Omelet.
DINNER.—Split-Pea Soup, Oyster Crab Patties, Pike, Fresh Boiled Beef, Lettuce Salad, Brie Cheese, Apple Pie.
SUPPER.—Veal Cutlets, Sheep's Feet, Crab Salad, American Cream Cheese, Strawberries and Cake.

TUESDAY 17th.

BREAKFAST.—Shad, Mutton Chops, Fresh Calf's Tongues, Eggs on Toast.
DINNER.—Ox-Tail Soup, Young Rabbit Pie, Fresh Cod Fish, Roast Beef, Water Cress Salad, Gruyere Cheese, Green Currant Pie.
SUPPER.—Mutton Stew, Bacon and Eggs Boiled Beef Salad, Munster Cheese, Strawberries and Cake.

WEDNESDAY 18th.

BREAKFAST.—Blue Fish, Veal Cutlets, Tripe, Ham and Eggs.
DINNER.—Shelled Bean Soup, Chicken Croquettes, Ray. Leg of Mutton, Lettuce Salad, Schweizer Cheese, Custard Pie.
SUPPER.—Meat Croquettes, Calf's Feet, Sardines, Potato Salad, Emmenthal Cheese, Strawberries and Cake.

THURSDAY 19th.

BREAKFAST.—Boiled Weak Fish, Beefsteak, Calf's Brains, Boiled Eggs.
DINNER.—Little Neck Clams, Onion Soup, Sweet-bread Patties, Shad, Chicken, Lettuce Salad, American Cream Cheese, Strawberry Short Cake.
SUPPER.—Veal Stew, Cold Ham, Omelet, Chicken Salad, Roquefort Cheese, Sliced Oranges and Cake.

FRIDAY 20th.

BREAKFAST.—Fish Croquettes, Flounders, Boiled Herrings, and Fried Eggs.
DINNER.—Clam Chowder, Devilled Crabs, Fresh Salmon, Mixed Salad, Neufchatel Cheese, Rice Pudding.
SUPPER.—Terrapin, Macaroni, Eggs on Toast, Herring Salad, Camembert Cheese, Strawberries and Cake.

SATURDAY 21st.

BREAKFAST.—Shad, Mutton Chops, Smoked Beef Tongue, Omelet.
DINNER.—Julienne Soup, Fresh Beef Tongue, Black Bass, Roast Veal, Lettuce Salad, Cheese Pie.
SUPPER.—Meat Croquettes, Pickled Mackerel, Potato Salad, Muster Cheese, Strawberries and Cake.

SUNDAY 22d.

BREAKFAST.—Shrimps Patties, Liver and Bacon, Sweet-breads, Eggs.
DINNER.—Little Neck Clams, Beef Soup, Vole-au-vent, Sheep's Head, Fish, Chicken, Cos Salad, Roquefort Cheese, Plum Pudding, Ice Cream.
SUPPER.—Chicken Croquettes, Meat Jelly, Lobster Salad, Parmesant Cheese, Sliced Pine Apple and Cake.

JUNE, MONDAY 23d.

BREAKFAST.—Boiled Fresh Mackerel, Beefsteak, Kidney, Omelet.
DINNER.—Split-Pea Soup, Calf's Head, Pike, Fresh Boiled Beef, Lettuce Salad,
Brie Cheese, Apple Pie.
SUPPER.—Veal Cutlets, Sheep's Feet, Cold Ham, Water Cress Salad, American
Cream Cheese, Strawberries and Cake.

TUESDAY 24th.

BREAKFAST.—Shad, Mutton Chops, Fresh Calf's Tongues, Eggs on Toast.
DINNER.—Pepper Pot, Young Rabbit Pie, Fresh Cod Fish, Roast Beef, Mixed
Salad, Gruyere Cheese, Mince Meat Pie.
SUPPER.—Mutton Stew, Omelet, Cold Ham. Boiled Beef Salad, Munster Cheese,
Strawberries and Cake.

WEDNESDAY 25th.

BREAKFAST.—Blue Fish, Broiled Veal Cutlets, Ham and Eggs.
DINNER.—Shelled-Bean Soup, Chicken Croquettes, White Fish, Leg of !Mutton,
Cole Slaw, Schweizer Cheese, Custard Pie.
SUPPER.—Meat Croquettes, Eggs on Toast, Smoked Beef Tongue, Fresh Fish Salad,
Emmenthal Cheese, Strawberries and Cake.

THURSDAY 26th.

BREAKFAST.—Boiled Weak Fish, Beefsteak, Calf's Brains, Omelet.
DINNER.—Little Neck Clams, Onion Soup, Sweet-bread Patties, Shad, Chicken,
Lettuce Salad, American Cream Cheese, Strawberry Short Cake.
SUPPER.—Veal Stew, Sheep's Feet, Chicken Salad, Roquefort Cheese, Sliced
Oranges and Cake.

FRIDAY 27th.

BREAKFAST.—Fish Croquettes, Yellow Cat Fish, Boned Herrings and Fried Eggs.
DINNER.—Turtle Soup, Devilled Crabs, Cured Cod Fish, String Bean Salad,
Neufchatel Cheese, Apple Dumplings.
SUPPER.—Clam Fritters, Macaroni, Eggs on Toast, Herring Salad, Camembert Cheese,
Strawberries and Cake.

SATURDAY 28th.

BREAKFAST.—Shad, Mutton Chops, Tripe, Omelet.
DINNER.—Julienne Soup, Fresh Beef Tongue, Haddock, Sour Kraut and Pork,
Lettuce Salad, Cheese Pie.
SUPPER.—Meat Croquettes, Pickled Salmon, Potato Salad, Munster Cheese, Straw-
berries and Cake.

SUNDAY 29th.

BREAKFAST.—Shrimp Patties, Liver and Bacon, Sweet-breads, Eggs.
DINNER.—Little Neck Clams, Beef Soup, Vole-au-vent, Fresh Lake Trout, Boiled
Ham, Cos Salad, Roquefort Cheese, Plum Pudding, Ice Cream.
SUPPER.—Chicken Croquettes, Meat Jelly, Lobster Salad, Parmesant Cheese, Sliced
Pine Apple and Cake.

JUNE, MONDAY 30th.

BREAKFAST.—Boiled Fresh Mackerel, Beefsteak, Kidneys, Omelet.
DINNER.—Split-Pea Soup, Spring Chicken Patties, Pike, Corned Beef, Lettuce Salad, Brie Cheese, Apple Pie.
SUPPER.—Veal Cutlets, Young Rabbit Pie, Asparagus Salad, American Cream Cheese, Strawberries and Cake.

JULY.

TUESDAY 1st.

BREAKFAST.—Shad, Mutton Chops, Fresh Calf's Tongues, Eggs on Toast.
DINNER.—Veal Soup, Strasburg's Fat Liver Fresh Cod Fish, Roast Beef, Water Cress Salad, Gruyere Cheese, Stoned Cherry Pie.
SUPPER.—Mutton Stew, Omelet, Crab Salad, Munster Cheese, Strawberries and Cake.

WEDNESDAY 2d.

BREAKFAST.—Blue Fish, Veal Cutlets. Fresh Calf's Tongues, Boiled Eggs.
DINNER.—Shelled-Bean Soup, Chicken Croquettes, Rock Fish, Leg of Mutton, Mixed Salad, Schweizer Cheese, Mince Meat Pie.
SUPPER.—Meat Croquettes, Calf's Feet, Sardines, String Bean Salad, Emmenthal Cheese, Strawberries and Cake.

THURSDAY 3d.

BREAKFAST.—Boiled Weak Fish, Beefsteak. Calf's Brains, Omelet.
DINNER.—Little Neck Clams, Onion Soup. Sweet Bread Patties, Shad, Chicken, Lettuce Salad, American Cream Cheese, Strawberry Short Cake.
SUPPER.—Veal Stew, Sheep's Feet, Chicken Salad, Roquefort Cheese, Sliced Oranges and Cake.

FRIDAY 4th.

BREAKFAST.—Fish Croquettes, King Fish, Boned Herrings and Fried Eggs.
DINNER.—Clam Chowder, Devilled Crabs, Cured Cod Fish, Cole Slaw, Neufchatel Cheese, Rice Pudding.
SUPPER.—Oyster Crab Patties, Macaroni, Eggs on Toast, Herring Salad, Camembert Cheese, Strawberries and Cake.

SATURDAY 6th.

BREAKFAST.—Shad, Mutton Chops, Tripe, Omelet.
DINNER.—Julienne Soup, Calf's Head, Sheep's Head Fish, Roast Lamb, Lettuce Salad, Cheese Pie.
SUPPER.—Meat Croquettes, Pickled Salmon, Potato Salad, Munster Cheese, Stoned Cherry and Cake.

SUNDAY 6th.

BREAKFAST.—Shrimps Patties, Liver and Bacon, Sweet-breads, Eggs.
DINNER.—Little Neck Clams, Beef Soup, Vole-au-vent, Black Bass, Chicken, Cos Salad, Roquefort Cheese, Plum Pudding, Ice Cream.
SUPPER.—Chicken Croquettes, Meat Jelly, Lobster Salad, Parmesant Cheese, Sliced Pine Apple and Cake.

JULY, MONDAY 7th.

BREAKFAST.—Boiled Fresh Mackerel, Beefsteak, Kidneys, Omelet.
DINNER.—Split-Pea Soup, Calf's Feet, Pike, Fresh Boiled Beef, Lettuce Salad, Brie Cheese, Apple Pie.
SUPPER.—Veal Cutlets, Bacon and Eggs, Anchovy Salad, American Cream Cheese, Currant Jelly and Cake.

TUESDAY 8th.

BREAKFAST.—Shad, Mutton Chops, Fresh Calf's Tongues, Eggs on Toast.
DINNER.—Pepper Pot, Chicken Patties, Fresh Cod Fish, Roast Beef, Cole Slaw, Gruyere Cheese, Strawberry Short Cake.
SUPPER.—Mutton Stew, Omelet, Boiled Beef Salad, Munster Cheese, Prunes and Cake.

WEDNESDAY 9th.

BREAKFAST.—Blue Fish, Veal Cutlets, Ham and Eggs.
DINNER.—Shelled Bean Soup, Sweet Bread Patties, Rock Fish, Leg of Mutton, Water Cress Salad, Schweizer Cheese, Stoned Cherry Pie.
SUPPER.—Meat Croquettes, Sheep's Feet, Fresh Fish Salad, Emmenthal Cheese, Blackberry Jelly and Cake.

THURSDAY 10th.

BREAKFAST.--Weak Fish, Beefsteak, Chicken Croquettes, Eggs.
DINNER.—Little Neck Clams, Onion Soup, Oyster Crab Patties, Shad, Chicken, Lettuce Salad, American Cream Cheese, Mince Meat Pie.
SUPPER.—Veal Stew, Omelet, Smoked Beef Salad, Chicken Salad, Roquefort Cheese, Sliced Oranges and Cake.

FRIDAY 11th.

BREAKFAST.—Fish Croquettes, Cod Fish Tongues, Flounders, Boned Herrings and Fried Eggs.
DINNER.—Bouille-a-Baisse, Devilled Crabs, Ray, String Bean Salad, Neufchatel Cheese, Apple Dumplings.
SUPPER.—Clam Fritters, Macaroni, Fried Brook Trout, Eggs on Toast, Herring Salad, Camembert Cheese, Raspberry Jelly and Cake.

SATURDAY 12th.

BREAKFAST.—Shad, Mutton Chops, Calf's Brains, Omelet.
DINNER.—Julienne Soup, Tripe, Halibut, Roast Veal, Lettuce Salad, Cheese Pie.
SUPPER.—Meat Croquettes, Pickled Mackerel, Potato Salad, Muster Cheese, Cranberry Jelly and Cake.

SUNDAY 13th.

BREAKFAST.—Shrimps Patties, Liver and Bacon, Sweet-breads, Eggs.
DINNER.—Little Neck Clams, Beef Soup, Vole-au-vent, Fresh Salmon, Chicken, Cos Salad, Roquefort Cheese, Plum Pudding, Ice Cream.
SUPPER.—Chicken Croquettes, Meat Jelly, Lobster Salad, Parmesant Cheese, Sliced Pine Apple and Cake.

JULY, MONDAY 14th.

BREAKFAST.—Boiled Fresh Mackerel, Beefsteak, Kidneys, Omelet.
DINNER.—Split-Pea Soup, Sheep's Feet, Pike, Fresh Boiled Beef, Lettuce Salad, Brie Cheese, Apple Pie.
SUPPER.—Veal Cutlets, Bacon and Eggs, Cold Smoked Tongue, Asparagus Salad, American Cream Cheese, Prunes and Cake.

TUESDAY 15th.

BREAKFAST.—Shad, Mutton Chops, Fresh Calf's Tongues, Eggs on Toast.
DINNER.—Ox-Tail Soup, Calf's Brains, Fresh Cod Fish, Roast Beef, Cole Slaw, Gruyere Cheese, Currant Pie.
SUPPER.—Mutton Stew, Tripe, Omelet, Crab Salad, Munster Cheese, Quince Marmalade and Cake.

WEDNESDAY 16th.

BREAKFAST.—Blue Fish, Veal Cutlets, Young Rabbit Patties, Eggs.
DINNER.—Shelled Bean Soup, Chicken Croquettes, White Perch, Leg of Mutton, Water Cress Salad, Schweizer Cheese, Custard Pie.
SUPPER.—Meat Croquettes, Eggs on Toast, Sardines, Potato Salad, Emmenthal Cheese, Blackberries and Cake.

THURSDAY 17th.

BREAKFAST.—Weak Fish, Beefsteak, Giblet's Patties, Omelet.
DINNER.—Little Neck Clams, Onion Soup, Sweet-bread Patties, Shad, Chicken, Lettuce Salad, American Cream Cheese, Apricot Tart.
SUPPER.—Veal Stew, Fresh Beef's Tongue, Cold Ham, Chicken Salad, Roquefort Cheese, Sliced Oranges and Cake.

FRIDAY 18th.

BREAKFAST.—Fish Croquettes, Yellow Cat Fish, Boned Herrings and Fried Eggs.
DINNER.—Clam Soup, Devilled Crabs, Fresh Salmon, String Bean Salad, Neufchatel Cheese, Rice Pudding.
SUPPER.—Oyster Crab Patties, Macaroni, Eggs on Toast, Herring Salad, Munster Cheese, Huckelberries and Cake.

SATURDAY 19th.

BREAKFAST.—Shad, Mutton Chops, Ham and Eggs.
DINNER.—Julienne Soup, Strasburg's Fat Liver, Black Bass, Beef-a-la-mode, Lettuce Salad, Cheese Pie.
SUPPER.—Meat Croquettes, Pickled Salmon, Potato Salad, Camembert Cheese, Currant Jelly and Cake.

SUNDAY 20th.

BREAKFAST.—Shrimps Patties, Liver and Bacon, Sweet-breads, Eggs.
DINNER.—Little Neck Clams, Beef Soup, Vole-au-vent, Sheep's Head, Fish, Filet of Beef, Cos Salad, Roquefort Cheese, Plum Pudding, Ice Cream.
SUPPER.—Chicken Croquettes, Meat Jelly, Lobster Salad, Parmesant Cheese, Sliced Pine Apple and Cake.

JULY, MONDAY 21st.

BREAKFAST.—Boiled Fresh Mackerel, Beefsteak, Kidneys, Omelet.
DINNER.—Split-Pea Soup, Strasburg Fat Liver, Fresh Boiled Beef, Lettuce Salad, Brie Cheese, Apple Pie.
SUPPER.—Veal Cutlets, Bacon and Eggs, Asparagus Salad, American Cream Cheese, Quince Marmalade and Cake.

TUESDAY 22d.

BREAKFAST.—Shad, Mutton Chops, Fresh Calf's Tongues, Eggs on Toast.
DINNER.—Veal Soup, Young Rabbit Patties, Fresh Cod Fish, Roast Beef, Water Cress Salad, Gruyere Cheese, Currant Jelly Pie.
SUPPER.—Mutton Stew, Giblet's Pie, Omelet, Boiled Beef Salad, Munster Cheese, Stoned Cherries and Cake.

WEDNESDAY 23d.

BREAKFAST.—Blue Fish, Veal Cutlets, Ham and Eggs.
DINNER.—Shelled Bean Soup, Chicken Croquettes, White Fish, Leg of Mutton, Mixed Salad, Schweizer Cheese, Apricot Tart.
SUPPER.—Meat Croquettes, Eggs, Tripe, Fresh Fish Salad, Emmenthal Cheese, Raspberry Jelly and Cake.

THURSDAY 24th.

BREAKFAST.—Boiled Weak Fish, Beefsteak Calf's Brains. Omelet.
DINNER.—Little Neck Clams, Onion Soup, Sweet-bread Patties, Shad, Chicken, Lettuce Salad, American Cream Cheese, Mince Meat Pie.
SUPPER.—Veal Stew, Smoked Beef's Tongue, Chicken Salad, Roquefort Cheese, Sliced Oranges and Cake.

FRIDAY 25th.

BREAKFAST.—Fish Croquettes, Yellow Perch, Boned Herrings, and Fried Eggs.
DINNER.—Clam Soup, Devilled Crabs, Cured Cod Fish, String Bean Salad Neufchatel Cheese, Apple Dumplings.
SUPPER.—Terrapin, Macaroni, Eggs on Toast, Herring Salad, Munster Cheese, Prunes and Cake.

SATURDAY 26th.

BREAKFAST.—Shad, Mutton Chops, Sheep's Feet, Omelet.
DINNER.—Julienne Soup, Fresh Beef Tongue, Fresh Salmon, Roast Veal, Lettuce Salad, Cheese Pie.
SUPPER.—Meat Croquettes, Cold Ham, Pickled Mackerel, Potato Salad, Camembert Cheese, Blackberries and Cake.

SUNDAY 27th.

BREAKFAST.—Shrimp Patties, Liver and Bacon, Sweet-breads, Eggs.
DINNER.—Little Neck Clams, Beef Soup, Vole-au-vent, Salmon Trout, Chicken, Cos Salad, Roquefort Cheese, Plum Pudding, Ice Cream.
SUPPER.—Chicken Croquettes, Meat Jelly, Lobster Salad, Parmesant Cheese, Sliced Pine Apple and Cake.

33

JULY, MONDAY 28th.

BREAKFAST.—Boiled Fresh Mackerel, Beefsteak, Kidneys, Omelet.
DINNER.—Split-Pea Soup, Oyster Crab Patties, Pike, Fresh Boiled Beef, Lettuce Salad, Brie Cheese, Apple Pie.
SUPPER.—Veal Cutlets, Cold Ham, Calf's Feet, Eggs, Asparagus Salad, American Cream Cheese, Prunes and Cake.

TUESDAY 29th.

BREAKFAST.—Shad, Mutton Chops, Fresh Calf's Tongues, Eggs on Toast.
DINNER.—Veal Soup, Young Rabbit Patties, Fresh Cod Fish, Roast Beef, Water Cress Salad, Gruyere Cheese, Stoned Cherry Pie.
SUPPER.—Mutton Stew, Bacon and Eggs, Crab Salad, Munster Cheese, Raspberry Jelly and Cake.

WEDNESDAY 30th.

BREAKFAST.—Blue Fish, Veal Cutlets, Ham and Eggs.
DINNER.—Shelled-Bean Soup, Chicken Croquettes, Rock Fish, Leg of Mutton, Cole Slaw, Schweizer Cheese, Custard Pie.
SUPPER.—Meat Croquettes, Omelet, Sardines, Potato Salad, Emmenthal Cheese, Cranberry Jelly and Cake.

THURSDAY 31st.

BREAKFAST.—Boiled Weak Fish, Beefsteak, Calf's Brains, Omelet.
DINNER.—Little Neck Clams, Onion Soup, Sweet Bread Patties, Shad, Chicken, Lettuce Salad, American Cream Cheese, Mince Meat Pie.
SUPPER.—Veal Stew, Sheep's Feet, Eggs, Chicken Salad, Roquefort Cheese, Sliced Oranges and Cake.

AUGUST.

FRIDAY 1st.

BREAKFAST.—Fish Croquettes, Yellow Perch, Boned Herrings and Fried Eggs.
DINNER.—Clam Soup, Devilled Crabs, Cured Cod Fish, String Bean Salad, Neufchatel Cheese, Rice Pudding.
SUPPER.—Cod Tongue Fritters, Macaroni, Eggs on Toast, Herring Salad, Munster Cheese, Quince Marmalade and Cake.

SATURDAY 2d.

BREAKFAST.—Shad, Mutton Chops, Tripe, Omelet.
DINNER.—Julienne Soup, Fresh Beef's Tongue, Sheep's Head Fish, Roast Lamb, Lettuce Salad, Cheese Pie.
SUPPER.—Meat Croquettes, Pickled Salmon, Potato Salad, Camembert Cheese, Apple Jelly and Cake.

SUNDAY 3d.

BREAKFAST.—Shrimps Patties, Liver and Bacon, Sweet-breads, Eggs.
DINNER.—Little Neck Clams, Beef Soup, Vole-au-vent, Black Bass, Young Ducks, Cos Salad, Roquefort Cheese, Plum Pudding, Ice Cream.
SUPPER.—Chicken Croquettes, Meat Jelly, Lobster Salad, Parmesant Cheese, Sliced Pine Apple and Cake.

AUGUST, MONDAY 4th.

BREAKFAST.—Boiled Fresh Mackerel, Beefsteak, Kidneys, Omelet.
DINNER.—Split-Pea Soup, Squab Patties, Pike, Corned Beef, Lettuce Salad, Brie Cheese, Apple Pie.
SUPPER.—Veal Cutlets, Bacon and Eggs, Anchovy Salad, American Cream Cheese, Currant Jelly and Cake.

TUESDAY 5th.

BREAKFAST.—King Fish, Mutton Chops, Fresh Calf's Tongues, Eggs on Toast.
DINNER.—Ox-tail Soup, Young Duck Patties, Fresh Cod Fish, Roast Beef, Cole Slaw, Gruyere Cheese, Raspberry Jelly Pie.
SUPPER.—Mutton Stew, Calf's Feet, Boiled Beef Salad, Munster Cheese, Apricot Marmalade and Cake.

WEDNESDAY 6th.

BREAKFAST.—Blue Fish, Broiled Veal Cutlets, Ham and Eggs.
DINNER.—Shelled Bean Soup, Chicken Croquettes, Rock Fish, Leg of Mutton, Water Cress Salad, Schweizer Cheese, Stoned Cherry Pie.
SUPPER.—Meat Croquettes, Sheep's Feet, Eggs, Fresh Fish Salad, Emmenthal Cheese, Prunes and Cake.

THURSDAY 7th.

BREAKFAST.—Weak Fish, Beefsteak, Calf's Brains, Omelet.
DINNER.—Little Neck Clams, Onion Soup, Sweet Bread Patties, Fresh Salmon, Chicken, Lettuce Salad, American Cream Cheese, Mince Meat Pie.
SUPPER.—Veal Stew, Soft Shell Crabs, Eggs on Toast, Herring Salad, Munster Cheese, Sliced Oranges and Cake.

FRIDAY 8th.

BREAKFAST.—Fish Croquettes, Smelts, Boned Herrings and Fried Eggs.
DINNER.—Clam Soup, Devilled Crabs, Cured Cod Fish, String Bean Salad, Neufchatel Cheese, Apple Dumplings.
SUPPER.—Oyster Crab Patties, Macaroni, Brook Trout, Herring Salad, Munster Cheese, Cranberry Jelly and Cake.

SATURDAY 9th.

BREAKFAST.—Boiled Fresh Tongues, Mutton Chops, Tripe, Omelet.
DINNER.—Veal Soup, Young Rabbit Pie, Black Bass, Roast Veal, Lettuce Salad, Cheese Pie.
SUPPER.—Meat Croquettes, Pickled Mackerel, Potato Salad, Camembert Cheese, Quince Marmalade and Cake.

SUNDAY 10th.

BREAKFAST.—Shrimps Patties, Liver and Bacon, Sweet-breads, Eggs.
DINNER.—Little Neck Clams, Beef Soup, Vole-au-vent, Sheep's Head Fish, Chicken, Cos Salad, Roquefort Cheese, Plum Pudding, Ice Cream.
SUPPER.—Chicken Croquettes, Meat Jelly, Lobster Salad, Parmesant Cheese, Sliced Pine Apple and Cake.

AUGUST, MONDAY 11th.

BREAKFAST.--Boiled Fresh Mackerel, Beefsteak, Kidneys, Omelet.
DINNER.—Split-Pea Soup, Sheep's Feet, Pike, Fresh Boiled Beef, Lettuce Salad, Brie Cheese, Apple Pie.
SUPPER.—Veal Cutlets, Young Duck Pie, Eggs, Water Cress Salad, American Cream Cheese, Cranberry Jelly and Cake.

TUESDAY 12th.

BREAKFAST.—Yellow Cat Fish, Mutton Chops, Fresh Veal's Tongues, Eggs.
DINNER.—Ox-Tail Soup, Calf's Feet, Fresh Cod Fish, Roast Beef, Cole Slaw, Gruyere Cheese, Peach Pie.
SUPPER.—Mutton Stew, Omelet, Bacon and Fried Eggs, Shrimp Patties, Munster Cheese, Apple Jelly and Cake.

WEDNESDAY 13th.

BREAKFAST.—Boiled Blue Fish, Broiled Veal Cutlets, Ham and Eggs.
DINNER.—Shelled Bean Soup, Chicken Croquettes, Ray, Leg of Mutton, Mixed Salad, Schweizer Cheese, Currant Jelly Pie.
SUPPER.—Meat Croquettes, Omelet, Squab's Pie, Crab Salad, Emmenthal Cheese, Prunes and Cake.

THURSDAY 14th.

BREAKFAST.—Boiled Weak Fish, Beefsteak, Calf's Brains, Boiled Eggs.
DINNER.—Little Neck Clams, Onion Soup, Sweet-bread Patties, White Fish, Chicken, Lettuce Salad, American Cream Cheese, Mince Meat Pie.
SUPPER.—Veal Stew, Eggs, Sardines, Chicken Salad, Roquefort Cheese, Sliced Oranges and Cake.

FRIDAY 15th.

BREAKFAST.—Fish Croquettes, Brook Trout, Boned Herrings and Fried Eggs.
DINNER.—Oyster Soup, Devilled Crabs, Garfish, String Bean Salad, Munster Cheese, Rice Pudding.
SUPPER.—Clam Fritters, Macaroni, Eggs on Toast, Herring Salad, Neufchatel Cheese, Apricot Marmalade and Cake.

SATURDAY 16th.

BREAKFAST.—King Fish, Mutton Chops, Tripe, Omelet.
DINNER.—Julienne Soup, Calf's Head, Black Bass, Beef-a-la-mode, Lettuce Salad, Cheese Pie.
SUPPER.—Meat Croquettes, Pickled Salmon, Potato Salad, Camembert Cheese, Sliced Peaches and Cake.

SUNDAY 17th.

BREAKFAST.—Shrimps Patties, Liver and Bacon, Sweet-breads, Eggs.
DINNER.—Little Neck Clams, Beef Soup, Vole-au-vent, Sheep's Head, Fish, Filet of Beef, Cos Salad, Roquefort Cheese, Plum Pudding, Ice Cream.
SUPPER.—Chicken Croquettes, Meat Jelly, Lobster Salad, Parmesant Cheese, Sliced Pine Apple and Cake.

AUGUST, MONDAY 18th.

BREAKFAST.—Boiled Fresh Mackerel, Beefsteak, Kidneys, Omelet.
DINNER.—Split-Pea Soup, Tripe, Pike, Fresh Boiled Beef, Lettuce Salad, Brie Cheese,
Apple Pie.
SUPPER.—Veal Cutlets, Young Duck Pie, Bacon and Eggs, Water Cress Salad,
American Cream Cheese, Sliced Peaches and Cake.

TUESDAY 19th.

BREAKFAST.—King Fish, Mutton Chops, Fresh Calf's Tongues, Eggs on Toast.
DINNER.—Pepper Pot, Oyster Crab Patties, Fresh Cod Fish, Roast Beef, Cole Slaw,
Gruyere Cheese, Currant Jelly Pie.
SUPPER.—Mutton Stew, Squab Pie, Omelet, Boiled Beef Salad, Munster Cheese,
Prunes and Cake.

WEDNESDAY 20th.

BREAKFAST.—Boiled Blue Fish, Broiled Veal Cutlets, Ham and Eggs.
SDINNER.—Shelled Bean Soup, Chicken Croquettes, White Fish, Leg of Mutton,
Mixed Salad, Schweizer Cheese, Peach Pie.
SUPPER.—Meat Croquettes, Sheep's Feet, Omelet, Fresh Fish Salad, Emmenthal
Cheese, Stoned Cherry Pie.

THURSDAY 21st.

BREAKFAST.—Boiled Weak Fish, Beefsteak, Calf's Brains. Omelet.
DINNER.—Little Neck Clams, Onion Soup, Sweet-bread Patties, Rock Fish, Chicken,
Lettuce Salad, American Cream Cheese, Mince Meat Pie.
SUPPER.—Veal Stew, Fresh Beef's Tongue, Chicken Salad, Roquefort Cheese, Sliced
Oranges and Cake.

FRIDAY 22d.

BREAKFAST.—Fish Croquettes, Bull Frog Legs, Boned Herrings, and Fried Eggs.
DINNER.—Oyster Soup, Devilled Crabs, Cured Cod Fish, String Bean Salad, Neuf-
chatel Cheese, Apple Dumplings.
SUPPER.—Clam Fritters, Macaroni, Eggs on Toast, Herring Salad, Munster Cheese,
Sliced Peaches and Cake.

SATURDAY 23d.

BREAKFAST.—Flounders, Broiled Mutton Chops, Tripe, Omelet.
DINNER.—Julienne Soup, Squab Patties, Halibut. Young Goose, Lettuce Salad,
Cheese Pie.
SUPPER.—Meat Croquettes, Pickled Mackerel, Potato Salad, Camembert Cheese,
Apricot Marmalade and Cake.

SUNDAY 24th.

BREAKFAST.—Shrimps Patties, Liver and Bacon, Sweet-breads, Eggs.
DINNER.—Little Neck Clams, Beef Soup, Vole-au-vent, Salmon Trout, Roast of Fat
Veal, Cos Salad, Roquefort Cheese, Plum Pudding, Ice Cream.
SUPPER.—Chicken Croquettes, Meat Jelly, Lobster Salad, Parmesant Cheese, Sliced
Pine Apple and Cake.

AUGUST, MONDAY 25th.

BREAKFAST.—Boiled Fresh Mackerel, Beefsteak, Kidneys, Omelet.
DINNER.—Split-Pea Soup, Young Rabbit Pie, Pike, Fresh Boiled Beef, Lettuce Salad, Brie Cheese, Apple Pie.
SUPPER.—Veal Cutlets, Calf's Brains, Bacon and Eggs, Water Cress Salad, Sliced Peaches and Cake.

TUESDAY 26th.

BREAKFAST.—King Fish, Mutton Chops, Fresh Calf's Tongues, Eggs on Toast.
DINNER.—Ox-tail Soup, Young Duck Pie, Fresh Cod Fish, Roast Beef, Cole Slaw, Gruyere Cheese, Peach Pie.
SUPPER.—Mutton Stew, Tripe, Omelet, Corn Salad, Munster Cheese, Currant Jelly and Cake.

WEDNESDAY 27th.

BREAKFAST.—Blue Fish, Broiled Veal Cutlets. Sheep's Feet, Ham and Eggs.
DINNER.—Shelled Bean Soup, Chicken Croquettes, Garfish, Leg of Mutton, Water Cress Salad, Schweizer Cheese, Stoned Cherry Pie.
SUPPER.—Meat Croquettes, Squab's Pie, Crab Salad, Emmenthal Cheese, Sliced Peaches and Cake.

THURSDAY 28th.

BREAKFAST.—Weak Fish, Beefsteak, Oyster Crab Patties, Boiled Eggs.
DINNER.—Little Neck Clams, Onion Soup, Sweet-bread Patties, Ray, Chicken, Lettuce Salad, American Cream Cheese, Peach Pie.
SUPPER.—Veal Stew, Omelet, Sardines, Chicken Salad, Roquefort Cheese, Sliced Oranges and Cake.

FRIDAY 29th.

BREAKFAST.—Fish Croquettes, Flounders, Boned Herrings and Fried Eggs
DINNER.—Oyster Soup, Devilled Crabs, Cured Cod Fish, String Bean Salad, Neufchatel Cheese, Rice Pudding
SUPPER.—Clam Fritters, Macaroni, Eggs on Toast, Herring Salad, Munster Cheese, Sliced Peaches.

SATURDAY 30th.

BREAKFAST.—Cod Tongues, Broiled Mutton Chops, Sheep's Feet, Omelet.
DINNER.—Julienne Soup, Young Ducks, Sheep's Head Fish, Roast Lamb, Lettuce Salad, Cheese Pie.
SUPPER.—Meat Croquettes, Pickled Mackerel, Potato Salad, Camembert Cheese, Sliced Peaches.

SUNDAY 31st.

BREAKFAST.—Shrimps Patties, Liver and Bacon, Sweet-breads, Eggs.
DINNER.—Little Neck Clams, Beef Soup, Vole-au-vent, Black Bass, Chicken, Cos Salad, Roquefort Cheese, Plum Pudding, Ice Cream.
SUPPER.—Chicken Croquettes, Meat Jelly, Lobster Salad, Parmesant Cheese, Sliced Pine Apple and Cake.

SEPTEMBER.

MONDAY 1st.

BREAKFAST.—Boiled Fresh Mackerel, Beefsteak, Kidneys, Omelet.
DINNER.—Split-Pea Soup, Oyster Crab Patties, Corned Beef, Lettuce Salad, Brie Cheese, Apple Pie.
SUPPER.—Veal Cutlets, Bacon and Eggs, Anchovy Salad, American Cream Cheese, Sliced Peaches and Cake.

TUESDAY 2d.

BREAKFAST.—King Fish, Mutton Chops, Fresh Calf's Tongues, Eggs on Toast.
DINNER.—Veal Soup, Squab Pie, Fresh Cod Fish, Roast Beef, Cole Slaw, Gruyere Cheese, Apricot Tart.
SUPPER.—Mutton Stew, Tripe, Omelet, Boiled Beef Salad, Munster Cheese, Sliced Peaches and Cake.

WEDNESDAY 3d.

BREAKFAST.—Blue Fish, Broiled Veal Cutlets, Ham and Eggs.
DINNER.—Shelled-Bean Soup, Chicken Croquettes, Rock Fish, Leg of Mutton, Water Cress Salad, Schweizer Cheese, Peach Pie.
SUPPER.—Meat Croquettes, Sheep's Feet, Eggs, Crab Salad, Emmenthal Cheese, Stoned Cherries and Cake.

THURSDAY 4th.

BREAKFAST.—Boiled Weak Fish, Beefsteak, Fresh Beef's Tongue, Eggs.
DINNER.—Little Neck Clams, Onion Soup, Sweet-bread Patties, White Fish, Lettuce Salad, Mince Meat Pie.
SUPPER.—Veal Stew, Omelet, Chicken Salad, Roquefort Cheese, Sliced Oranges and Cake.

FRIDAY 5th.

BREAKFAST.—Fish Croquettes, Yellow Cat Fish, Boned Herrings and Fried Eggs.
DINNER.—Oyster Soup, Devilled Crabs, Cured Cod Fish, String Bean Salad, Neufchatel Cheese, Apple Dumplings.
SUPPER.—Clam Fritters, Macaroni, Eggs on Toast, Herring Salad, Munster Cheese, Sliced Peaches and Cake.

SATURDAY 6th.

BREAKFAST.—Eels, Broiled Mutton Chops, Calf's Brains, Omelet.
DINNER.—Julienne Soup, Reed Birds, Haddock, Roast Veal, Lettuce Salad, Cheese Pie.
SUPPER.—Meat Croquettes, Eggs, Pickled Salmon, Potato Salad, Camembert Cheese, Currant Jelly and Cake.

SUNDAY 7th.

BREAKFAST.—Shrimp Patties, Liver and Bacon, Sweet-breads, Eggs.
DINNER.—Little Neck Clams, Beef Soup, Vole-au-vent, Fresh Salmon, Young Ducks, Cos Salad, Roquefort Cheese, Plum Pudding, Ice Cream.
SUPPER.—Chicken Croquettes, Meat Jelly, Lobster Salad, Parmesant Cheese, Sliced Pine Apple and Cake.

SEPTEMBER, MONDAY 8th.

BREAKFAST.—Boiled Fresh Mackerel, Beefsteak, Kidneys, Omelet.

DINNER.—Split-Pea Soup, Reed Birds, Pike, Fresh Boiled Beef, Lettuce Salad, Brie Cheese, Apple Pie.

SUPPER.—Fried Oysters, Calf's Feet, Head Cheese, Water Cress Salad, American Cream Cheese, Sliced Peaches and Cake.

TUESDAY 9th.

BREAKFAST.—King Fish, Mutton Chops, Fresh Beef's Tongues, Eggs on Toast.

DINNER.—Ox-Tail Soup, Oyster Crab Patties, Fresh Cod Fish, Roast Beef, Cole Slaw, Gruyere Cheese, Peach Pie.

SUPPER.—Mutton Stew, Bacon and Eggs, Corn Salad, Munster Cheese, Stoned Cherries and Cake.

WEDNESDAY 10th.

BREAKFAST.—Blue Fish, Broiled Veal Cutlets, Ham and Eggs.

DINNER.—Shelled Bean Soup, Chicken Croquettes, Ray, Leg of Mutton, Corn Salad, Schweizer Cheese, Currant Jelly Pie.

SUPPER.—Meat Croquettes, Sheep s Feet, Crab Salad, Emmenthal Cheese, Sliced Peaches and Cake.

THURSDAY 11th.

BREAKFAST.--Boiled Weak Fish, Beefsteak, Sausage, Omelet.

DINNER.—Oysters on shell, Onion Soup, Sweet Bread Patties, White Fish, Chicken, Lettuce Salad, American Cream Cheese, Mince Meat Pie.

SUPPER.—Veal Stew, Eggs, Sardines, Chicken Salad, Roquefort Cheese, Sliced Peaches and Cake.

FRIDAY 12th.

BREAKFAST.—Fish Croquettes, Brook Trout, Boned Herrings, and Fried Eggs.

DINNER.—Oyster Soup, Devilled Crabs, Cured Cod Fish, String Bean Salad, Neufchatel Cheese, Rice Pudding.

SUPPER.—Clam Fritters, Macaroni, Eggs, Herring Salad, Munster Cheese, Raspberry Jelly and Cake.

SATURDAY 13th.

BREAKFAST.—Flounders, Mutton Chops, Fresh Calf's Tongues, Omelet.

DINNER.—Julienne Soup, Oyster Patties, Black Bass, Beef-a-la-mode, Lettuce Salad, Cheese Pie.

SUPPER.—Meat Croquettes, White Sausage, Pickled Salmon, Potato Salad, Camembert Cheese, Sliced Peaches and Cake.

SUNDAY 14th.

BREAKFAST.—Shrimps Patties, Liver and Bacon, Sweet-breads, Eggs.

DINNER.—Oysters on shell, Beef Soup, Vole-au-vent, Sheep's Head, Fish, Filet of Beef, Cos Salad, Roquefort Cheese, Plum Pudding, Ice Cream.

SUPPER.—Chicken Croquettes, Meat Jelly, Lobster Salad, Parmesant Cheese, Sliced Pine Apple and Cake.

SEPTEMBER, MONDAY 15th.

BREAKFAST.—Boiled Fresh Mackerel, Beefsteak, Kidneys, Omelet.
DINNER.—Split-Pea Soup, Pig's Feet, Pike, Fresh Boiled Beef, Lettuce Salad, Brie Cheese, Apple Pie.
SUPPER.—Fried Oysters, Young Rabbit Pie, Head Cheese, Water Crese Salad, Sliced Peaches and Cake.

TUESDAY 16th.

BREAKFAST.—King Fish, Mutton Chops, Fresh Calf's Tongues, Eggs on Toast.
DINNER.—Turtle Soup, Reed Birds, Fresh Cod Fish, Roast Beef, Endive Salad, Gruyere Cheese, Peach Pie.
SUPPER.—Mutton Stew, Bacon and Eggs, Boiled Beef Salad, Munster Cheese, Prunes and Cake.

WEDNESDAY 17th.

BREAKFAST.—Blue Fish, Broiled Veal Cutlets, Ham and Eggs.
DINNER.—Shelled Bean Soup, Chicken Croquettes, Rock Fish, Leg of Mutton, Water Cress Salad, Schweizer Cheese, Custard Pie.
SUPPER.—Meat Croquettes, Eggs, Calf's Feet, Crab Salad, Emmenthal Cheese, Sliced Peaches and Cake.

THURSDAY 18th.

BREAKFAST.—Weak Fish, Beefsteak, Sausage, Boiled Eggs.
DINNER.—Oysters on shell, Onion Soup, Sweet Bread Patties, White Fish, Chicken, Lettuce Salad, American Cream Cheese, Mince Meat Pie.
SUPPER.—Veal Stew, Strasburg Fat Liver, Omelet, Chicken Salad, Roquefort Cheese, Sliced Oranges and Cake.

FRIDAY 19th.

BREAKFAST.—Fish Croquettes, Yellow Perch, Boned Herrings and Fried Eggs.
DINNER.—Oyster Soup, Devilled Crabs, Cured Cod Fish, String Bean Salad, Neufchatel Cheese, Apple Dumplings.
SUPPER.—Clam Fritters, Macaroni, Eggs on Toast, Herring Salad, Munster Cheese, Sliced Peaches and Cake.

SATURDAY 20th.

BREAKFAST.—Cod Tongues, Eels, Pork Steak, Calf's Brains, Omelet.
DINNER.—Julienne Soup, Oyster Patties, Halibut, Roast Veal, Lettuce Salad, Cheese Pie.
SUPPER.—Meat Croquettes, Sausage, Eggs, Pickled Mackerel, Potato Salad, Camembert Cheese, Sliced Oranges and Cake.

SUNDAY 21st.

BREAKFAST.—Shrimps Patties, Liver and Bacon, Sweet-breads, Eggs.
DINNER.—Oysters on shell, Beef Soup, Vole-au-vent, Salmon Trout, Chicken, Cos Salad, Roquefort Cheese, Plum Pudding, Ice Cream.
SUPPER.—Chicken Croquettes, Meat Jelly, Lobster Salad, Parmesant Cheese, Sliced Pine Apple and Cake.

SEPTEMBER, MONDAY 22d.

BREAKFAST.—Boiled Fresh Mackerel, Beefsteak, Kidneys, Omelet.
DINNER.—Split-Pea Soup, Reed Birds, Pike, Fresh Boiled Beef, Lettuce Salad, Brie Cheese, Apple Pie.
SUPPER.—Fried Oysters, Young Duck Pie, Head Cheese, Water Cress Salad, American Cream Cheese, Sliced Peaches.

TUESDAY 23d.

BREAKFAST.—Yellow Cat Fish, Mutton Chops, Fresh Beef's Tongues, Eggs.
DINNER.—Clam Soup, Pig's Feet, Fresh Cod Fish, Roast Beef, Endive Salad, Gruyere Cheese. Peach Pie.
SUPPER.—Mutton Stew, Bacon and Eggs, Fresh Fish Salad, Munster Cheese, Stoned Cherries and Cake.

WEDNESDAY 24th.

BREAKFAST.—Blue Fish, Broiled Veal Cutlets, Ham and Eggs.
DINNER.—Shelled Bean Soup, Chicken Croquettes, Garfish, Leg of Mutton, Cole Slaw, Schweizer Cheese, Peach Pie.
SUPPER.—Meat Croquettes, White Sausage, Cold Ham, Crab Salad, Emmenthal Cheese, Prunes and Cake.

THURSDAY 25th.

BREAKFAST.—Weak Fish, Beefsteak, Sausage, Boiled Eggs.
DINNER.—Oysters on shell, Onion Soup, Rail Birds, White Fish, Chicken, Lettuce Salad, American Cream Cheese, Mince Meat Pie.
SUPPER.—Veal Stew, Omelet, Sardines, Chicken Salad, Roquefort Cheese, Sliced Oranges and Cake.

FRIDAY 26th.

BREAKFAST.—Fish Croquettes, Eels, Boned Herrings and Fried Eggs.
DINNER.—Oyster Soup, Devilled Crabs, Cured Cod Fish, String Bean Salad, Neufchatel Cheese, Rice Pudding.
SUPPER.—Clam Fritters, Macaroni, Eggs on Toast, Herring Salad, Munster Cheese, Sliced Peaches and Cake.

SATURDAY 27th.

BREAKFAST.—Brook Trout, Cod Tongues, Pork Steak, Sheep's Feet, Omelet.
DINNER.—Julienne Soup, Oyster Patties, Sheep's Head Fish, Roast Lamb, Lettuce Salad, Cheese Pie.
SUPPER.—Meat Croquettes, Rail Birds, Venison, Pickled Salmon, Potato Salad, Camembert Cheese, Currant Jelly and Cake.

SUNDAY 28th.

BREAKFAST.—Shrimps Patties, Liver and Bacon. Sweet-breads, Eggs
DINNER.—Oysters on shell, Beef Soup, Vole-au-vent, Black Bass, Partridges, Cos Salad, Roquefort Cheese, Plum Pudding. Ice Cream.
SUPPER.—Chicken Croquettes, Meat Jelly, Lobster Salad, Parmesant Cheese, Sliced Pine Apple and Cake.

SEPTEMBER, MONDAY 29th.

BREAKFAST.—Boiled Fresh Mackerel, Beefsteak, Kidneys, Omelet.

DINNER.—Split-Pea Soup, Squab Patties, Pike, Corned Beef, Lettuce Salad, Brie Cheese, Apple Pie.

SUPPER.—Fried Oysters, Sausage, Eggs, Anchovy Salad, American Cream Cheese, Sliced Peaches and Cake.

TUESDAY 30th.

BREAKFAST.—King Fish, Mutton Chops, Fresh Calf's Tongues, Eggs on Toast.

DINNER.—Clam Soup, Young Duck Pie, Fresh Cod Fish, Roast Beef, Corn Salad, Gruyere Cheese, Peach Pie.

SUPPER.—Mutton Stew, Bacon and Eggs, Boiled Beef Salad, Munster Cheese, Stoned Cherries and Cake.

OCTOBER.

WEDNESDAY 1st.

BREAKFAST.—Blue Fish, Broiled Veal Cutlets, Sausages, Boiled Eggs.

DINNER.—Shelled Bean Soup, Chicken Croquettes, Rock Fish, Leg of Mutton, Water Cress Salad, Schweizer Cheese, Currant Jelly Pie.

SUPPER.—Meat Croquettes, Pudding Sausage, Sheep's Feet, Crab Salad, Emmenthal Cheese, Sliced Peaches and Cake.

THURSDAY 2d.

BREAKFAST.—Weak Fish, Beefsteak, Reed Birds, Boiled Omelet.

DINNER.—Oysters on shell, Onion Soup, White Fish, Chicken, Lettuce Salad, American Cream Cheese, Mince Meat Pie.

SUPPER.—Veal Stew, Sausage, Chicken Salad, Roquefort Cheese, Sliced Oranges and Cake.

FRIDAY 3d.

BREAKFAST.—Fish Croquettes, Flounders, Boned Herrings and Fried Eggs.

DINNER.—Oyster Soup, Devilled Crabs, Cured Cod Fish, String Bean Salad, Neuf-chatel Cheese, Apple Dumplings.

SUPPER.—Clam Fritters, Macaroni, Eggs on Toast, Herring Salad, Munster Cheese, Sliced Peaches and Cake.

SATURDAY 4th.

BREAKFAST.—Yellow Cat Fish, Broiled Veal Steak, Ham and Eggs.

DINNER.—Julienne Soup, Oyster Patties, Haddock, Roast Pork, Lettuce Salad, Cheese Pie.

SUPPER.—Meat Croquettes, Sausage, Pickled Mackerel, Potato Salad, Camembert Cheese, Prunes and Cake.

SUNDAY 5th.

BREAKFAST.—Shrimps Patties, Liver and Bacon, Sweet-breads, Eggs.

DINNER.—Oysters on shell, Beef Soup, Vole-au-vent, Fresh Salmon. Turkey, Corn Salad, Roquefort Cheese, Plum Pudding, Ice Cream.

SUPPER.—Chicken Croquettes, Meat Jelly, Lobster Salad, Parmesant Cheese, Sliced Pine Apple and Cake.

OCTOBER, MONDAY 6th.

BREAKFAST.—Boiled Fresh Mackerel, Beefsteak, Kidneys, Omelet.
DINNER.—Split-Pea Soup, Reed Birds, Pike, Fresh Boiled Beef, Lettuce Salad, Brie Cheese, Apple Pie.
SUPPER.—Fried Oysters, Sausage, Head Cheese, Corn Salad, American Cream Cheese, Raspberry Jelly and Cake.

TUESDAY 7th.

BREAKFAST.—Caviar, King Fish, Mutton Chops, Sausage, Eggs.
DINNER.—Ox-tail Soup, Fresh Calf's Tongues, Fresh Cod Fish, Roast Beef, Endivo Salad, Gruyere Cheese, Currant Jelly Pie.
SUPPER.—Hare Pie, Bacon and Eggs, Calf's Brains, Water Cress Salad, Munster Cheese, Prunes and Cake.

WEDNESDAY 8th.

BREAKFAST.—Blue Fish, Veal Cutlets, Rail Birds, Omelet.
DINNER.—Shelled Bean Soup, Chicken Croquettes, White Perch, Leg of Mutton, Cole Slaw, Schweizer Cheese, Custard Pie.
SUPPER.—Meat Croquettes, White Sausage, Eggs on Toast, Crab Salad, Emmenthal Cheese, Stoned Cherries and Cake.

THURSDAY 9th.

BREAKFAST.—Weak Fish, Beefsteak, Sausage, Boiled Eggs.
DINNER.—Oysters on shell, Onion Soup, Sweet-bread Patties, White Fish, Chicken, Lettuce Salad, American Cream Cheese, Mince Meat Pie.
SUPPER.—Broiled Pork Steak, Sardines, Chicken Salad, Roquefort Cheese, Sliced Oranges and Cake.

FRIDAY 10th.

BREAKFAST.—Fish Croquettes, Brook Trout, Boned Herrings and Fried Eggs
DINNER.—Oyster Soup, Devilled Crabs, Cured Cod Fish, String Bean Salad, Neuf chatel Cheese, Rice Pudding.
SUPPER.—Clam Fritters, Macaroni, Eggs on Toast, Herring Salad, Munster Cheese. Cranberry Jelly and Cake.

SATURDAY 11th.

BREAKFAST.—Scallops, Broiled Pork Steak, Quails, Ham and Eggs.
DINNER.—Julienne Soup, Oyster Patties, Black Bass, Beef-a-la-mode, Lettuce Salad, Cheese Pie.
SUPPER.—Meat Croquettes, Sausage, Venison, Pickled Mackerel, Potato Salad. Camembert Cheese, Raspberry Jelly and Cake.

SUNDAY 12th.

BREAKFAST.—Shrimps Patties, Liver and Bacon, Sweet-breads, Eggs.
DINNER.—Oysters on shell, Beef Soup, Vol-au-vent, Sheep's Head Fish, Canvas-back Ducks, Cos Salad, Roquefort Cheese, Plum Pudding, Ice Cream.
SUPPER.—Chicken Croquettes, Meat Jelly, Lobster Salad, Parmesant Cheese, Sliced Pine Apple and Cake.

OCTOBER, MONDAY 13th.

BREAKFAST.—Boiled Fresh Mackerel, Beefsteak, Sausage, Omelet.

DINNER.—Split-Pea Soup, Kidneys, Pike, Fresh Boiled Beef, Corn Salad, Brie Cheese, Apple Pie.

SUPPER.—Fried Oysters, Head Cheese, Bacon and Eggs, Calf's **Brains**, Water Cress Salad, American Cream Cheese, Stewed Pears and Cake.

TUESDAY 14th.

BREAKFAST.—King Fish, Mutton Chops, Pig's Liver, Reed Birds, Eggs.

DINNER.—Turtle Soup, Oyster Crab Patties, Fresh Cod Fish, Roast Beef, Cole Slaw, Gruyere Cheese, Squash Pie.

SUPPER.—Pork Steak, Rabbit Pie, Omelet, Boiled Beef Salad, Munster Cheese, Quince Marmalade and Cake.

WEDNESDAY 15th.

BREAKFAST.—Blue Fish, Broiled Veal Cutlets, Sausage, Ham and Eggs.

DINNER.—Shelled-Bean Soup, Chicken Croquettes, Ray, Leg of Mutton, Lettuce Salad, Schweizer Cheese, Cocoanut Pie.

SUPPER.—Meat Croquettes, Calf's Feet, Eggs, Crab Salad, Emmenthal Cheese, Currant Jelly and Cake.

THURSDAY 16th.

BREAKFAST.—Weak Fish, Beefsteak, Sheep's Feet, Omelet.

DINNER.—Oysters on shell, Onion Soup, Sweet-bread Patties, White Fish, Chicken, Lettuce Salad, American Cream Cheese, Mince Meat Pie.

SUPPER.—Pig's Feet, Fresh Beef's Tongue, Sausage, Chicken Salad, Roquefort Cheese, Sliced Oranges and Cake.

FRIDAY 17th.

BREAKFAST.—Fish Croquettes, Flounders, Boned Herrings and Fried Eggs.

DINNER.—Oyster Soup, Devilled Crabs, Cured Cod Fish, String Bean Salad, Munster Cheese, Apple Dumplings.

SUPPER.—Clam Fritters, Macaroni, Eggs on Toast, Herring Salad, Neufchatel Cheese, Roasted Chestnuts, Apple Jelly and Cake.

SATURDAY 18th.

BREAKFAST.—Yellow Perch, Broiled Porksteak, Ham and Eggs.

DINNER.—Julienne Soup, Oyster Patties, Halibut. Roast Veal, Corn Salad, Cheese Pie.

SUPPER.—Meat Croquettes, Sausage, Pickled Mackerel, Potato Salad, Camembert Cheese, Stoned Cherries and Cake.

SUNDAY 19th.

BREAKFAST.—Shrimps Patties, Liver and Bacon, Sweet-breads, Eggs.

DINNER.—Oysters on shell, Beef Soup, Vol-au-vent, Fresh Salmon, Wood Cocks, Lettuce Salad, Roquefort Cheese, Plum Pudding, Ice Cream.

SUPPER.—Chicken Croquettes, Meat Jelly, Lobster Salad, Parmesaut Cheese, Sliced Pine Apple and Cake.

OCTOBER, MONDAY 20th.

BREAKFAST.—Boiled Fresh Mackerel, Beefsteak, Sausage, Omelet.
DINNER.—Split-Pea Soup, Reed Birds, Pike, Fresh Boiled Beef, Corn Salad, Brie Cheese, Apple Pie.
SUPPER.—Fried Oysters, Pig's Feet, Bacon and Eggs, Water Cress Salad, American Cream Cheese, Prunes and Cake

TUESDAY 21st.

BREAKFAST.—King Fish, Mutton Chops, Head Cheese, Eggs on Toast.
DINNER.—Veal Stew, Snipes, Fresh Cod Fish, Roast Beef, Endive Salad, Gruyere Cheese, Custard Pie.
SUPPER.—Wild Duck Pie, Kidneys, Omelet, Fresh Fish Salad, Munster Cheese, Stewed Prunes and Cake.

WEDNESDAY 22d.

BREAKFAST.—Blue Fish, Veal Cutlets, Fresh Beef's Tongue, Boiled Eggs.
DINNER.—Shelled Bean Soup, Chicken Croquettes, Garfish, Leg of Mutton, Scorzonera Sprouts Salad, Schweizer Cheese, Currant Jelly Pie.
SUPPER.—Meat Croquettes, Woodcock Pie, Crab Salad, Emmenthal Cheese, Raspberry Jelly and Cake.

THURSDAY 23d.

BREAKFAST.—Weak Fish, Beefsteak, Sausage, Omelet.
DINNER.—Oysters on shell, Onion Soup, Sweet Bread Patties, White Fish, Chicken, Lettuce Salad, American Cream Cheese, Mince Meat Pie.
SUPPER.—Hare Pie, White Sausage, Sardines, Chicken Salad, Roquefort Cheese, Sliced Oranges and Cake.

FRIDAY 24th.

BREAKFAST.—Fish Croquettes, Scallops, Boned Herrings and Fried Eggs.
DINNER.—Oyster Soup, Devilled Crabs, Cured Cod Fish, String Bean Salad, Neufchatel Cheese, Rice Pudding.
SUPPER.—Clam Fritters, Macaroni, Eggs on Toast, Herring Salad, Munster Cheese, Roasted Chestnuts, Cranberry Jelly and Cake.

SATURDAY 25th.

BREAKFAST.—Cod Tongues, Brook Trout, Pork Steak, Quails, Ham and Eggs.
DINNER.—Julienne Soup, Oyster Patties, Sheep's Head Fish, Sour Kraut and Pork, Cheese Pie.
SUPPER.—Meat Croquettes, Sausage, Venison, Pickled Salmon, Potato Salad, Camembert Cheese, Apple Jelly and Cake.

SUNDAY 26th.

BREAKFAST.—Shrimps Patties, Liver and Bacon, Sweet-breads, Eggs.
DINNER.—Oysters on shell, Beef Soup, Vole-au-vent, Black Bass, Wild Goose, Lettuce Salad, Roquefort Cheese, Plum Pudding, Ice Cream.
SUPPER.—Chicken Croquettes, Meat Jelly, Lobster Salad, Parmesant Cheese, Sliced Pine Apple and Cake.

OCTOBER, MONDAY 27th.

BREAKFAST.—Boiled Fresh Mackerel, Beefsteak, Sausage, Omelet.

DINNER.—Split-Pea Soup, Pigeon Pie, Pike, Fresh Boiled Beef, Cole Slaw, Brie Cheese, Apple Pie.

SUPPER.—Fried Oysters, Calf's Feet, Bacon and Eggs, Anchovy Salad, American Cream Cheese, Stewed Pears and Cake.

TUESDAY 28th.

BREAKFAST.—King Fish, Beefsteak, Fresh Calf's Tongues, Eggs on Toast.

DINNER.—Ox-Tail Soup. Partridge Patties, Fresh Cod Fish, Roast Beef, Lettuce Salad, Gruyere Cheese, Apricot Tart.

SUPPER.—Mutton Stew, Sausage, Omelet, Crab Salad, Munster Cheese, Prunes and Cake.

WEDNESDAY 29th.

BREAKFAST.—Blue Fish, Veal Cutlets, Sheep's Feet, Ham and Eggs.

DINNER.—Shelled Bean Soup, Chicken Croquettes, Rock Fish, Leg of Mutton, CornSalad, Schweizer Cheese, Stoned Cherry Pie.

SUPPER.—Meat Croquettes, Boned Wild Rabbit Pie, Omelet, Sardines, Potato Salad, Schweizer Cheese, Raspberry Jelly and Cake.

THURSDAY 30th.

BREAKFAST.—Weak Fish. Beefsteak, Sausage, Boiled Eggs.

DINNER.—Oysters on shell, Onion Soup, Sweet Bread Patties, White Fish, Chicken, Lettuce Salad, American Cream Cheese, Mince Meat Pie.

SUPPER.—Woodcock Pie, Sheep's Feet, Bacon and Eggs, Chicken Salad, Roquefort Cheese, Sliced Oranges and Cake.

FRIDAY 31st.

BREAKFAST.—Fish Croquettes, Yellow Perch, Boned Herrings and Fried Eggs.

DINNER.—Oyster Soup, Devilled Crabs, Cured Cod Fish, String Bean Salad, Neufchatel Cheese, Apple Dumplings.

SUPPER.—Clam Fritters, Macaroni, Eggs on Toast, Herring Salad, Munster Cheese, Chestnuts, Blackberry Jelly and Cake.

NOVEMBER.

SATURDAY 1st.

BREAKFAST.—Flounders, Pork Steak, Tripe, Scrambled Eggs.

DINNER.—Julienne Soup, Oyster Patties, Haddock, Roast Lamb, Corn Salad, Cheese Pie.

SUPPER.—Meat Croquettes, Sausage, Pickled Mackerel, Potato Salad, Camembert Cheese, Apple Jelly and Cake.

SUNDAY 2d.

BREAKFAST.—Shrimps Patties, Liver and Bacon, Sweet-breads, Eggs.

DINNER.—Oysters on shell, Beef Soup, Vole-au-vent, Fresh Salmon, Turkey, Lettuce Salad, Roquefort Cheese, Plum Pudding, Ice Cream.

SUPPER.—Chicken Croquettes, Meat Jelly, Lobster Salad, Parmesant Cheese, Sliced Pine Apple and Cake.

47

NOVEMBER, MONDAY 3d.

BREAKFAST.—Boiled Fresh Mackerel, Beefsteak, Sausage, Omelet.
DINNER.—Split-Pea Soup, Reed Birds, Pike, Corned Beef, Corn Salad, Brie Cheese, Apple Pie.
SUPPER.—Fried Oysters, Kidneys, Bacon and Eggs, Succory Salad, American Cream Cheese, Stewed Pears and Cake.

TUESDAY 4th.

BREAKFAST.—Yellow Cat Fish, Mutton Chops, Scrappel, Eggs on Toast.
DINNER.—Clam Soup, Pigeons Pie, Fresh Cod Fish, Roast Beef, Cole Slaw, Gruyere Cheese, Squash Pie.
SUPPER.—Venison, Sausage, Quails, Boiled Beef Salad, Munster Cheese, Prunes and Cake.

WEDNESDAY 5th.

BREAKFAST.—Blue Fish, Veal Cutlets. Fresh Beef's Tongue, Ham and Eggs.
DINNER.—Shelled Bean Soup, Chicken Croquettes, Rock Fish, Leg of Mutton, Turnip Sprouts Salad, Schweizer Cheese, Custard Pie.
SUPPER.—Meat Croquettes, Jugged Hare, Eggs, Crab Salad, Emmenthal Cheese, Raspberry Jelly and Cake.

THURSDAY 6th.

BREAKFAST.—Weak Fish, Beefsteak, Calf's Brains, Sausage, Omelet.
DINNER.—Oysters on shell, Onion Soup, Sweet-bread Patties. Salmon Trout, Chicken Endive Salad, American Cream Cheese, Mince Meat Pie.
SUPPER.—Veal Stew, Sausage, Sardines, Chicken Salad, Roquefort Cheese, Sliced Oranges and Cake.

FRIDAY 7th.

BREAKFAST.—Fish Croquettes. Eels, Boned Herrings and Fried Eggs.
DINNER.—Oyster Soup, Devilled Crabs, Cured Cod Fish, String Bean Salad, Neufchatel Cheese, Rice Pudding
SUPPER.—Clam Fritters, Macaroni, Eggs on Toast, Herring Salad, Munster Cheese, Roasted Chestnuts, Cranberry Jelly and Cake.

SATURDAY 8th.

BREAKFAST.—King Fish, Broiled Pork Steak, Snipes, Omelet.
DINNER.—Julienne Soup, Oyster Patties, Black Bass, Wild Ducks, Water Cress Salad, Cheese Pie.
SUPPER.—Meat Croquettes, Sausage, Pickled Mackerel, Potato Salad, Camembert Cheese, Prunelle Marmalade and Cake.

SUNDAY 9th.

BREAKFAST.—Shrimps Patties, Liver and Bacon, Sweet-breads, Eggs.
DINNER.—Oysters on shell, Beef Soup, Vol-au-vent, Sheep's Head Fish, Woodcocks, Lettuce Salad, Roquefort Cheese, Plum Pudding, Ice Cream.
SUPPER.—Chicken Croquettes, Meat Jelly, Lobster Salad, Parmesant Cheese, Sliced Pine Apple and Cake.

NOVEMBER, MONDAY 10th.

BREAKFAST.—Boiled Fresh Mackerel, Beefsteak, Sausage, Omelet.
DINNER.—Split-Pea Soup, Oyster Crab Patties, Pike, Fresh Boiled Beef, Cole Slaw, Brie Cheese, Apple Pie.
SUPPER.—Fried Oysters, Rail Birds, Head Cheese, Succory Salad, American Cream Cheese, Currant Jelly and Cake.

TUESDAY 11th.

BREAKFAST.—Scallops, Mutton Chops, Pig's Feet, Eggs on Toast.
DINNER.—Veal Soup, Tripe, Fresh Cod Fish, Roast Beef, Corn Salad, Gruyere Cheese, Apricot Tart.
SUPPER.—Veal Stew, Boned Wild Rabbit Pie, Bacon and Eggs, Red Cabbage Salad, Munster Cheese, Prunes and Cake.

WEDNESDAY 12th.

BREAKFAST.—Blue Fish, Veal Cutlets, Fresh Beef's Tongue, Eggs.
DINNER.—Shelled-Bean Soup, Chicken Croquettes, Ray, Leg of Mutton, Water Cress Salad, Schweizer Cheese, Cocoanut Pie.
SUPPER.—Meat Croquettes, Omelet, Strasburg Fat Liver, Potato Salad, Emmenthal Cheese, Raspberry Jelly and Cake.

THURSDAY 13th.

BREAKFAST.—Weak Fish, Beefsteak, Sausage, Quails, Eggs.
DINNER.—Oysters on shell, Onion Soup, Sweet-bread Patties, Garfish, Chicken, Lettuce Salad, American Cream Cheese, Mince Meat Pie.
SUPPER.—Woodcock Pie, Bacon and Eggs, Chicken Salad, Roquefort Cheese, Sliced Oranges and Cake.

FRIDAY 14th.

BREAKFAST.—Fish Croquettes, Yellow Fish, Boned Herrings and Fried Eggs.
DINNER.—Oyster Soup, Devilled Crabs, Cured Cod Fish, Scorzonera Sprouts Salad, Neufchatel Cheese, Apple Dumplings.
SUPPER.—Clam Fritters, Macaroni, Eggs on Toast, Herring Salad, Munster Cheese, Roasted Chestnuts, Stoned Cherries and Cake.

SATURDAY 15th.

BREAKFAST.—King Fish, Broiled Pork Steak, Sheep's Feet, Eggs on Toast.
DINNER.—Julienne Soup, Oyster Patties, Halibut, Beef-a-la-mode, Endive Salad, Cheese Pie.
SUPPER.—Meat Croquettes, Sausage, Pickled Mackerel, Potato Salad, Camembert Cheese, Apple Jelly and Cake.

SUNDAY 16th.

BREAKFAST.—Shrimps Patties, Liver and Bacon, Sweet-breads, Eggs.
DINNER.—Oysters on shell, Beef Soup, Vole-au-vent, Fresh Lake Trout, Canvas-back Ducks, Lettuce Salad, Roquefort Cheese, Plum Pudding, Ice Cream.
SUPPER.—Chicken Croquettes, Meat Jelly, Lobster Salad, Parmesant Cheese, Sliced Pine Apple and Cake.

NOVEMBER, MONDAY 17th.

BREAKFAST.—Boiled Fresh Mackerel, Beefsteak, Sausage, Omelet.

DINNER.—Split-Pea Soup, Snipes, Pike, Fresh Boiled Beef, Cole Slaw, Brie Cheese, Apple Pie.

SUPPER.—Fried Oysters, Kidneys, Head Cheese, Turnip Sprouts Salad, American Cream Cheese, Stewed Pears and Cake.

TUESDAY 18th.

BREAKFAST.—Eels, Mutton Chops, Pig's Feet, Trushes, Eggs.

DINNER.—Turtle Soup, Boned Wild Rabbit Pie, Fresh Cod Fish, Roast Beef, Corn Salad, Gruyere Cheese, Apricot Tart.

SUPPER.—Wild Pigeons, Sausage, Fresh Beef's Tongue, Omelet, Red Cabbage Salad, Munster Cheese, Quince Marmalade and Cake.

WEDNESDAY 19th.

BREAKFAST.—Blue Fish, Broiled Veal Cutlets, Sausage, Ham and Eggs.

DINNER.—Shelled Bean Soup, Chicken Croquettes, White Fish, Leg of Mutton, Scorzonera Sprouts Salad, Schweizer Cheese, Custard Pie.

SUPPER.—Meat Croquettes, Quails, Sheep's Feet, Crab Salad, Emmenthal Cheese, Raspberry Jelly and Cake.

THURSDAY 20th.

BREAKFAST.--Weak Fish, Beefsteak, Calf's Brains, Head Cheese, Omelet.

DINNER.—Oysters on shell, Onion Soup, Sweet Bread Patties, Rock Fish, Chicken, Endive Salad, American Cream Cheese, Mince Meat Pie.

SUPPER.—Partridges, Sausage, Sardines, Chicken Salad, Roquefort Cheese, Sliced Oranges and Cake.

FRIDAY 21st.

BREAKFAST.—Fish Croquettes, Flounders, Boned Herrings and Fried Eggs.

DINNER.—Oyster Soup, Devilled Crabs, Cured Cod Fish, Water Cress Salad, Neufchatel Cheese, Rice Pudding.

SUPPER.—Clam Fritters, Macaroni, Eggs on Toast, Herring Salad, Munster Cheese, Roasted Chestnuts, Stoned Cherries and Cake.

SATURDAY 22d.

BREAKFAST.—Cod Tongues, Broiled Pork Steak, Quails, Omelet.

DINNER.—Julienne Soup, Oyster Patties, Sheep's Head Fish, Roast Veal, Succory Salad, Cheese Pie.

SUPPER.—Meat Croquettes, Sausage, Venison, Pickled Salmon, Potato Salad, Camembert Cheese, Apple Jelly and Cake.

SUNDAY 23d.

BREAKFAST.—Shrimps Patties, Liver and Bacon, Sweet-breads, Eggs.

DINNER.—Oysters on shell, Beef Soup, Vol-au-vent, Black Bass, Wild Goose, Lettuce Salad, Roquefort Cheese, Plum Pudding, Ice Cream.

SUPPER.—Chicken Croquettes, Meat Jelly, Lobster Salad, Parmesant Cheese, Sliced Pine Apple and Cake.

NOVEMBER, MONDAY 24th.

BREAKFAST.—Boiled Fresh Mackerel. Beefsteak, Sausage, Omelet.

DINNER.—Split-Pea Soup, Reed Birds, Pike, Fresh Boiled Beef, Cole Slaw, Brie Cheese, Apple Pie.

SUPPER.—Fried Oysters, Fresh Beef's Tongue, Head Cheese, Anchovy Salad, American Cream Cheese, Stewed Pears and Cake.

TUESDAY 25th.

BREAKFAST.—King Fish, Mutton Chops, Pig's Feet, Scrapple, Eggs.

DINNER.—Clam Soup, Jugged Hare, Fresh Cod Fish, Roast Beef, Corn Salad, Gruyere Cheese, Apricot Tart.

SUPPER.—Mutton Stew, Quails, Bacon and Eggs, Boiled Beef Salad, Munster Cheese, Prunes and Cake.

WEDNESDAY 26th.

BREAKFAST.—Blue Fish, Veal Cutlets, Rail Birds, Sheep's Feet, Eggs.

DINNER.—Shelled Bean Soup, Chicken Croquettes, Rock Fish, Leg of Mutton, Water Cress Salad, Schweizer Cheese, Stoned Cherry Pie.

SUPPER.—Meat Croquettes, Wild Rabbit Pie, Sardines, Potato Salad, Emmenthal Cheese, Raspberry Jelly and Cake.

THURSDAY 27th.

BREAKFAST.—Weak Fish, Beefsteak, Sausage, Head Cheese, Omelet.

DINNER.—Oysters on shell, Onion Soup, Sweet Bread Patties, White Fish, Chicken, Succory Salad, American Cream Cheese, Mince Meat Pie.

SUPPER.—Woodcock Pie, Calf's Brains, Eggs on Toast, Chicken Salad, Roquefort Cheese, Sliced Oranges and Cake.

FRIDAY 28th.

BREAKFAST.—Fish Croquettes, Yellow Catfish, Boned Herrings and Fried Eggs.

DINNER.—Oyster Soup, Devilled Crabs, Cured Cod Fish, Shrimp Salad, Neufchatel Cheese, Apple Dumplings.

SUPPER.—Clam Fritters, Macaroni, Omelet, Herring Salad, Munster Cheese, Roasted Chestnuts, Cranberry Jelly and Cake.

SATURDAY 29th.

BREAKFAST.—Cod Tongues, Smelts, Pork Steak, Tripe, Poached Eggs.

DINNER.—Julienne Soup, Oyster Patties, Fresh Lake Trout, Sour Kraut and Pork, Endive Salad Cheese Pie.

SUPPER.—Meat Croquettes, Sausage, Pickled Mackerel, Potato Salad, Camembert Cheese, Apple Jelly and Cake.

SUNDAY 30th.

BREAKFAST.—Shrimps Patties, Liver and Bacon, Sweet-breads, Eggs.

DINNER.—Oysters on shell, Beef Soup, Vole-au-vent, Fresh Salmon, Turkey, Lettuce Salad, Roquefort Cheese, Plum Pudding, Ice Cream.

SUPPER.—Chicken Croquettes, Meat Jelly, Lobster Salad, Parmesant Cheese, Sliced Pine Apple and Cake.

DECEMBER.

MONDAY 1st.

BREAKFAST.—Boiled Fresh Mackerel, Beefsteak, Sausage, Omelet.
DINNER.—Split-Pea Soup, Wild Ducks, Pike, Corned Beef, Corn Salad, Brie Cheese, Apple Pie.
SUPPER.—Fried Oysters, Patridges, Head Cheese, Red Cabbage Salad, American Cream Cheese, Stewed Pears and Cake.

TUESDAY 2d.

BREAKFAST.—Yellow Cat Fish, Mutton Chops, Pig's Feet, Scrappel, Eggs on Toast.
DINNER.—Ox Tail Soup, Oysters Crab Patties, Fresh Cod Fish, Roast Beef, Cole Slaw, Gruyere Cheese, Currant Jelly Pie.
SUPPER.—Jugged Hare, Strasburg Fat Liver, Omelet, Crab Salad, Munster Cheese, Stoned Cherries and Cake.

WEDNESDAY 3d.

BREAKFAST.—Blue Fish, Veal Cutlets. Sausages, Ham and Eggs.
DINNER.—Shelled Bean Soup, Chicken Croquettes, Ray, Leg of Mutton, Turnips Sprouts Salad, Schweizer Cheese, Custard Pie.
SUPPER.—Meat Croquettes, White Sausage, Calf's Feet, Sardines, Potato Salad, Emmenthal Cheese, Prunes and Cake.

THURSDAY 4th.

BREAKFAST.—Weak Fish, Beefsteak, Quails, Boiled Eggs.
DINNER.—Oysters on shell, Onion Soup, Sweet-bread Patties, White Fish, Chicken, Endive Salad, American Cream Cheese, Mince Meat Pie.
SUPPER.—Kidneys, Wild Rabbit Pie, Bacon and Eggs, Chicken Salad, Roquefort Cheese. Sliced Oranges and Cake.

FRIDAY 5th.

BREAKFAST.—Fish Croquettes. Yellow Perch, Herrings and Fried Eggs.
DINNER.—Oyster Soup, Devilled Crabs, Cured Cod Fish, Scorzonera Sprouts, Neufchatel Cheese, Rice Pudding.
SUPPER.—Clam Fritters, Macaroni, Eggs on Toast, Herring Salad, Munster Cheese, Roasted Chestnuts, Apple Jelly and Cake.

SATURDAY 6th.

BREAKFAST.—Scallops, Broiled Pork Steak, Rail Birds, Omelet.
DINNER.—Julienne Soup, Oyster Patties, Black Bass, Roast Lamb, Succory Salad, Cheese Pie.
SUPPER.—Meat Croquettes, Venison, Sausage, Pickled Salmon, Potato Salad, Camembert Cheese, Green Winter Berries and Cake.

SUNDAY 7th.

BREAKFAST.—Shrimps Patties, Liver and Bacon, Sweet-breads, Eggs.
DINNER.—Oysters on shell, Beef Soup, Vol-au-vent, Sheep's Head, Canvas Back Ducks, Lettuce Salad, Roquefort Cheese, Plum Pudding, Ice Cream.
SUPPER.—Chicken Croquettes, Meat Jelly, Lobster Salad, Parmesant Cheese, Sliced Pine Apple and Cake.

DECEMBER, MONDAY 8th.

BREAKFAST.—Boiled Fresh Mackerel, Beefsteak, Sausage, Omelet.
DINNER.—Split-Pea Soup, Quails, Pike, Corned Beef, Corn Salad, Brie Cheese, Apple Pie.
SUPPER.—Fried Oysters, Wild Rabbit Pie, Bacon and Eggs, Water Cress Salad, American Cream Cheese, Stewed Pears and Cake.

TUESDAY 9th.

BREAKFAST.—King Fish, Mutton Chops, Fresh Calf's Tongues, Eggs.
DINNER.—Veal Soup, Oyster Crab Patties, Fresh Cod Fish, Roast Beef, Cole Sla·, Gruyere Cheese, Currant Jelly Pie.
SUPPER.—Partriges, Tripe, Sausages, Crab Salad, Munster Cheese, Prunes and Cake.

WEDNESDAY 10th.

BREAKFAST.—Boiled Blue Fish, Broiled Veal Cutlets, Ham and Eggs.
DINNER.—Shelled-Bean Soup, Chicken Croquettes, Ray, Leg of Mutton, Scorzonora, Sprouts Salad, Schweizer Cheese, Apricot Tart.
SUPPER.—Meat Croquettes, White Sausage, Sheep's Feet, Sardines, Potato Salad, Emmenthal Cheese, Raspberry Jelly and Cake.

THURSDAY 11th.

BREAKFAST.—Weak Fish, Beefsteak, Sausage, Head Cheese, Omelet.
DINNER.—Oysters on shell, Onion Soup, Sweet-bread Patties, Rockfish, Chicken, Endive Salad, American Cream Cheese, Mince Meat Pie.
SUPPER.—Jugged Hare, Fresh Beef's Tongue, Chicken Salad, Roquefort Cheese, Sliced Oranges and Cake.

FRIDAY 12th.

BREAKFAST.—Fish Croquettes, Flounders, Boned Herrings and Fried Eggs.
DINNER.—Oyster Soup, Devilled Crabs, Cured Cod Fish, Succory Salad, Neufchatel Cheese, Rice Pudding.
SUPPER.—Clam Fritters, Macaroni, Eggs on Toast, Herring Salad, Munster Cheese, Roasted Chestnuts, Cranberry Jelly and Cake.

SATURDAY 13th.

BREAKFAST.—Brook Trout, Broiled Pork Steak, Sheep's Feet, Omelet.
DINNER.—Julienne Soup, Oyster Patties, Black Bass, Roast Veal, Turnip Sprouts Salad, Cheese Pie.
SUPPER.—Meat Croquettes, Snipes, Sausage, Pickled Mackerel, Potato Salad, Camembert Cheese, Apple Jelly and Cake.

SUNDAY 14th.

BREAKFAST.—Shrimps Patties, Liver and Bacon, Sweet-breads, Eggs.
DINNER.—Oysters on shell, Beef Soup, Vole-au-vent, Sheep's Head, Woodcocks, Lettuce Salad, Roquefort Cheese, Plum Pudding, Ice Cream.
SUPPER.—Chicken Croquettes, Meat Jelly, Lobster Salad, Parmesant Cheese, Sliced Pine Apple and Cake.

DECEMBER, MONDAY 15th.

BREAKFAST.—Boiled Fresh Mackerel, Beefsteak, Sausage, Omelet.
DINNER.—Split-Pea Soup, Wild Ducks, Pike, Boiled Beef, Cole Slaw, Brie Cheese, Apple Pie.
SUPPER.—Fried Oysters, Venison, Sheep's Feet, Water Cress Salad, American Cream Cheese, Stewed Pears.

TUESDAY 16th.

BREAKFAST.—King Fish, Mutton Chops, Calf's Brains, Scrappel, Eggs.
DINNER.—Turtle Soup, Quails, Fresh Cod Fish, Roast Beef, Corn Salad, Gruyere Cheese, Currant Jelly Pie.
SUPPER.—Wild Rabbit Pie, Fresh Beef's Tongue, Sardines, Potato Salad, Munster Cheese, Prunes and Cake.

WEDNESDAY 17th.

BREAKFAST.—Blue Fish, Broiled Veal Cutlets, Sausage, Eggs.
DINNER.—Shelled Bean Soup, Chicken Croquettes, Garfish, Leg of Mutton, Scorzonera Sprouts Sala l, Schweizer Cheese, Custard Pie.
SUPPER.—Meat Croquettes, Wild Pigeons, Omelet, Crab Salad, Emmenthal Cheese, Raspberry Jelly and Cake.

THURSDAY 18th.

BREAKFAST.—Boiled Weak Fish, Beefsteak, Ham and Eggs.
DINNER.—Oysters on shell, Onion Soup, Sweet Bread Patties, Rock Fish, Chicken, Endive Salad, American Cream Cheese, Mince Meat Pie.
SUPPER.—Partridges, Sausage, Sheep's Feet, Chicken Salad, Roquefort Cheese. Sliced Oranges and Cake.

FRIDAY 19th.

BREAKFAST.—Fish Croquettes, Yellow Perch, Boned Herrings and Fried Eggs.
DINNER.—Oyster Soup, Devilled Crabs, Cured Cod Fish, Succory Salad, Neufchatel Cheese, Rice Pudding.
SUPPER.—Clam Fritters, Macaroni, Eggs on Toast, Herring Salad, Roasted Chestnuts, Quince Marmalade and Cake.

SATURDAY 20th.

BREAKFAST.—Scallops, Broiled Pork Steak, Rail Birds, Omelet.
DINNER.—Julienne Soup, Oyster Patties, Sheep's Head Fish, Beef-a-la-mode, Cheese Pie.
SUPPER.—Meat Croquettes, Quails, Pickled Salmon, Potato Salad, Camembert Cheese, Green Winter Berries and Cake.

SUNDAY 21st.

BREAKFAST.—Shrimps Patties, Liver and Bacon, Sweet-breads, Eggs.
DINNER.—Oysters on shell, Beef Soup, Vole-au-vent, Black Bass, Canvas-back Ducks. Lettuce Salad, Roquefort Cheese, Plum Pudding. Ice Cream.
SUPPER.—Chicken Croquettes, Meat Jelly, Lobster Salad, Parmesant Cheese, Sliced Oranges and Cake.

DECEMBER, MONDAY 22d.

BREAKFAST.—Boiled Fresh Mackerel, Beefsteak, Sausage, Omelet.
DINNER.—Split-Pea Soup, Quails, Pike, Fresh Boiled Beef, Cole Slaw, Brie Cheese Apple Pie.
SUPPER.—Fried Oysters, Prairie Chicken, Anchovy Salad, American Cream Cheese, Stewed Pears and Cake

TUESDAY 23d.

BREAKFAST.—King Fish, Mutton Chops, Scrappel, Ham and Eggs.
DINNER.—Clam Soup, Calf's Feet, Fresh Cod Fish, Roast Beef, Corn Salad, Gruyere Cheese, Blackberry Jelly Pie.
SUPPER.—Venison, Sausage, Omelet, Sardines, Potato Salad, Munster Cheese, Prunes and Cake.

WEDNESDAY 24th.

BREAKFAST.—Blue Fish, Veal Cutlets, Sausage, Head Cheese, Eggs.
DINNER.—Shelled Bean Soup, Chicken Croquettes, Rock Fish, Leg of Mutton, Scorzonera Sprouts Salad, Schweizer Cheese, Currant Jelly Pie.
SUPPER.—Meat Croquettes, Pig's Feet, Bacon and Eggs, Crab Salad, Emmenthal Cheese, Stoned Cherries and Cake.

THURSDAY 25th.

BREAKFAST.—Weak Fish, Beefsteak, Sausage, Head Cheese, Omelet.
DINNER.—Oysters on shell, Beef Soup, Sweet Bread Patties, White Fish, Turkey, Endive Salad, American Cream Cheese, Mince Meat Pie.
SUPPER.—Wild Ducks, Fresh Beef's Tongue, Chicken Salad, Roquefort Cheese, Sliced Oranges and Cake.

FRIDAY 26th.

BREAKFAST.—Fish Croquettes, Eels, Boned Herrings and Fried Eggs
DINNER.—Oyster Soup, Devilled Crabs, Cured Cod Fish, Succory Salad, Neufchatel Cheese, Apple Dumplings.
SUPPER.—Clam Fritters, Macaroni, Eggs on Toast, Herring Salad, Munster Cheese, Roasted Chestnuts, Quince Marmalade and Cake.

SATURDAY 27th.

BREAKFAST.—Cod Tongues, Pork Steak, Sheep's Feet, Scrappel Omelet.
DINNER.—Julienne Soup, Oyster Patties, Haddock, Roast Veal, Red Cabbage Salad, Cheese Pie.
SUPPER.—Meat Croquettes, Sausage, Snipes, Pickled Mackerel, Potato Salad, Camembert Cheese, Apple Jelly and Cake.

SUNDAY 28th.

BREAKFAST.—Shrimps Patties, Liver and Bacon, Sweet-breads, Eggs.
DINNER.—Oysters on shell, Beef Soup, Vole-au-vent, Fresh Salmon, Chicken, Lettuce Salad, Roquefort Cheese, Plum Pudding, Ice Cream.
SUPPER.—Chicken Croquettes, Meat Jelly, Lobster Salad, Parmesant Cheese, Sliced Oranges and Cake.

DECEMBER, MONDAY 29th.

BREAKFAST.—Boiled Fresh Mackerel, Beefsteak, Sausage, Omelet.
DINNER.—Split-Pea Soup, Kidneys, Pike, Fresh Boiled Beef, Corn Slaw, Brie Cheese, Apple Pie.
SUPPER.—Fried Oysters, Boned Wild Rabbit Pie, Fresh Beef's Tongue, Water Cress Salad, Stewed Pears and Cake.

TUESDAY 30th.

BREAKFAST.—Flounders, Mutton Chops, Quails, Scrapple, Eggs on Toast.
DINNER.—Ox-Tail Soup, Oyster Crab Patties, Fresh Cod Fish, Roast Beef, Corn Salad, Gruyere Cheese, Currant Jelly Pie.
SUPPER.—Young Goose, Sheep's Feet, Bacon and Eggs, Sardines and Potato Salad, Munster Cheese, Prunes and Cake.

WEDNESDAY 31st.

BREAKFAST.—Blue Fish, Veal Cutlets, Sausage, Ham and Eggs.
DINNER.—Shelled-Bean Soup, Chicken Croquettes, Salmon Trout, Leg of Mutton, Turnip Sprouts Salad, American Cream Cheese, Custard Pie.
SUPPER.—Meat Croquettes, Pig's Feet, Strasburg's Fat Liver, Crab Salad, Roquefort Cheese, Stoned Cherries and Cake.

———•◆•———

There will be added, to the next issue of this Diary, advertisements of all kinds, especially from houses dealing in Groceries, Provisions, Wines, and anything pertaining to the table and the household.

The immense circulation of this Diary makes it one of best mediums for advertising.

Our rates for advertising in all the issues, within six months, are as follows:

Per Line........................50 cents.
For a quarter of a page...............$2.75.
For half of a page....................5.25.
For a full page.......................10.00.

9783337124465